None But The Mad

Jack Fenix

chipmunkapublishing

the mental health publisher

All rights reserved, no part of this publication may be reproduced by any means, electronic, mechanical photocopying, documentary, film or in any other format without prior written permission of the publisher.

Published by

Chipmunkapublishing

PO Box 6872

Brentwood

Essex CM13 1ZT

United Kingdom

http://www.chipmunkapublishing.com

Copyright © Jack Fenix 2011

Chipmunkapublishing gratefully acknowledge the support of Arts Council England.

Introduction

My madness was the belief that I was supposed to save the world from a great tragedy looming over the horizon, that I would find superpowers and defeat great evil known only as the figure I call 'The Green Jacket'. For most of my life I could not accept that this was delusion and rarely spoke about it for fear of my delusions being contradicted. It wasn't until I was hit by post-traumatic stress disorder which drove me to drug addiction that mental health became a priority for me and my visions were uncovered as delusions. Messianic delusions, post-traumatic stress, depression and further psychotic delusions about conspiracies, I have been through a great deal of the madness that's out there and yet at times when I look at the world I still wonder why I am the only sane person here.

I wanted to write this book because my madness has been a gift at times as well as a curse, because I wanted to be a part of helping our view of mental health issues be reformed to the point where it no longer scares people into silence or ignorance. Finally because there is no person alive on this planet who is completely sane and those who suffer from mental health problems are no different from you and it could have so easily been and still so easily might be you. We need to see this for what it is, an illness. We no longer fear many illnesses because we can cure them and we can treat them, mental illness is one of the few treatable and perhaps curable sets of conditions that are still feared as if it were leprosy in the first century AD. This attitude needs to change and we all need to learn because ignorance not only blocks sufferers from finding their footing in life but when it strikes someone with prejudices it can even prevent them from finding treatment for something they can't accept they have. One in four people directly suffers from mental health problems at some stage in their life, that's over one billion people worldwide and yet it is the only issue of such great consequence to be so frequently ignored. Things need to change, I only hope that this book can do some good and that at the very least it won't be responsible for something bad.

Chapter 1: First Things First

I was crazy for a long time before I went insane, I grew up noticing that the way people treat each other is insane. We all want happiness, love and security yet to get those things we're quite willing to take them from others. It's insane, like someone deciding to poison the atmosphere over a 'foreign' continent thinking, "That'll show 'em!" We all breathe the same air, we all live in the same world. Much as poison released far away will eventually diffuse into the atmosphere and poison the entire world, so do hateful actions whether you see it or not eventually make things worse for everyone. That is Karma, meaning action but also consequence. I was seven years old when I saw this.

Being the only sane person on Earth has a way of making you crazy. A little western boy and completely oblivious to Buddhism I assumed that since no-one else I knew seemed to see it that I was the only one who knew. Seven years old and coming to the conclusion that I alone could save the world, I should've been raised in a temple by monks and never felt so alone as I did that day. I despaired not only to see that the world was a place of exploitation and hate, but that so few even care. This place is so wrong, there is something wrong here. Like a black hand that twisted our past, controlled our minds and manipulated our future. There was something so wrong I could feel it without knowing it was there, like the unknown variable without which the results of the simulation are massively different.

Whether I was right or not I don't know, but I didn't want to believe either that some people are just stupid, or that some people are just evil. Without some dark force controlling the world one of these things or both had to be true.

I remember at five years old when I was first framed for a crime I didn't commit. Another boy had bitten himself on the arm and told the teachers it was me. They checked my teeth with less than advanced forensics, looked at them and said, "Yup, that's him." As they dragged me off to the naughty corner I bellowed that I was innocent, I told them he did it to himself just to frame me, "The bite marks are upside down! The bite marks!"

This was another horrifying realisation, not only were people in authority often more interested in dossing about than finding out the truth and acting accordingly, not only did they sometimes punish the innocent, but sometimes a bastard will bite himself on the arm just to watch you suffer.

School was always hard, people were always playing cruel tricks on me and it often felt like the world was out to get me. The phrase, Those who study the Abyss are studied by the abyss, seemed all too relevant. I was on to it, I knew it's dirty little secret and evil was determined to stop me. Yes by the time I was seven I was already crazy but things got steadily worse. I remember the tricks the girls would play quite well, they were unbelievably cruel, the kind of thing you'd expect from one of those demons of terrible evil that only pretends to be a little girl. The trick was this, to see how gullible I was. They would come up to me and pretend they wanted to be my girlfriend only to tell me they thought I was disgusting if I told them I liked them. I guess they just wanted the insult to come from someone who could hurt me most after building up my hopes. I mean it's no fun trying to tear something down unless it's going to make a decent thud, I actually think that day there was an audible crack as my heart broke in two.

Well like I said before it gets worse, obviously I was hunted like an animal, I hid in bushes, I ran a lot. Everyone seemed to hate me and even when I had an older brother at the school instead of protecting me he just lead an elite squad of older boys all of whom got their jollies watching me cry. I felt like nobody loved me, nobody cared about me and nobody wanted to be my friend. In case you don't remember these things, short of an abusive father these are the worst things in the world to a young boy.

So there I was with everyone and everything in my life making me miserable and it didn't stop at home even after my parents divorced. My brothers were ever ready to keep up the bullying and there are few things more emasculating than being beaten up by your younger brother. School was still worse because it covered more areas of self-esteem but it would've been nice to escape from it at home instead of living in perpetual fear for fifteen years.

I was introduced to death quite early too, two in fact. There I was, two years old in a corridor looking more bleak and dreary than it usually did in the house with no fun, and my gran was stood in the corridor crying. That true and terrible weeping you only see when the most terrible things happen. My parents kept trying to tell me that granddad was just gone or asleep or whatever the hell kind of misdirecting gibberish, but I saw the way she wept, like her heart had been torn out. He wasn't gone or asleep. Something much worse it had to be, he was dead.

Death, pain, suffering, I have to agree once again with the Buddhists on this one, life is suffering or at least mine was. I was driven for years by a singular hope, the hope of a better life. A wife I would love and always treat right, children I would cherish and raise happy and contented. A beautiful house with a beautiful garden, a wonderful job and no more brutality. A simple dream I think we're all entitled to, somewhere over the rainbow, just not me.

I remember girls always told me that no-one would ever love me, after years of feeling like no-one would ever love me this hurt me deeply. I could never forget it and became even more desperate to find a girlfriend when I believed it could never happen. I needed the warmth and comfort, the love and affection and of course to be reassured that there was someone in this world who could love even me. I never really found that, all I found was the ability to deal with crushing loneliness by means of letting the part of myself that cared die off.

This was my sorry excuse for living, no love or affection just persecution and hate. Sure I had all the necessities to survive, food, shelter and clean water but it's not enough to survive, without something to live for that survival felt like bitter ash going down and the constant reminder in my mind that survival, my only victory in life, was just a temporary win and in the end I was going to die. I think most people take some comfort from having lived happy, from having known love, I had nothing to comfort me not even denial, just always being aware of the impermanence of my life and even our species as a whole. We were all going to die and everything we ever did would be forgotten. Our best chance for any kind of a legacy even if not remembered was to actually do something amazing while we had the chance to exist, the same thing that comforts most people in death, not a world government ruled by an Oligarchy, I'm sure that's pretty common in the grand scheme of things but something really spectacular. Maybe we could ascend to a higher plane of existence but it's probably been done before too, we had to achieve the impossible, that one bright moment in all our existence when even a distant and capricious overlord would notice us for just a second and think, "Wow!"

That was my true dream, if I couldn't make my life mean anything on a personal level I could at least try to improve things for everyone else in great, unexpected and previously unimagined ways. This never really panned out, I thought I could save the world or at least make it worthwhile by the time it turns to ash but in the end nobody cares about anything except for what's happening on X-factor tonight or who's getting evicted from the Big Brother house. People don't care what anything means anymore, they just care about what they personally can take from it. My perhaps noble vision had failed to take into account anyone else and had failed to see this is not a world of dreams and great expectations, it is a world of low-paying supermarket jobs, of getting by watching whatever is on telly and doesn't completely disappoint you and settling for the one person in all the world that doesn't completely hate you. The world will burn and there'll be nothing to show for it, but fuck the world, it doesn't deserve people who actually care.

Years of verbal and physical abuse, living in fear in my own home, always running for fear of being hurt. The fact is I have always lived on the run, a fugitive without a crime and I am just so tired of it all. I have fought long and hard just to live a normal life, but it never comes. I was clinically depressed at nine years old and I have the face of an old soldier at twenty three. I have been fighting too long and I'm tired. I've given up on all my dreams and without them I'm nothing but another stupid ape on a dust-ball of a planet in the hill-billy backwaters of a meaningless universe. We're all completely fucked.

Chapter 2: Heroes

When your father isn't the man you want to be he can't be your role model, the difficult part is finding someone or something that can. For me it was always heroes as it is for many of us.

There were many heroes whom I aspired to be like, Guy Fawkes still burned in effigies every year, called a traitor for being a hero willing to try to blow up Parliament and the corrupt bastards within, Che Guevara a man who while he may have executed many people including those little more than child soldiers he was fighting a war for freedom and equality and of course the death of anyone who didn't believe in his idea of socialism, he was a brutal bastard and taught me many lessons about compassion for those who are different by showing me who I'd become otherwise but what he didn't show me by counter-example was that you must be willing to fight, die and kill for what you believe in, something we no longer possess.

Whether the person was real or fictional, they were all heroes to me and more real than the shadows of people I encountered every day, they were the few who had one thing in common, saw something they loved being destroyed and had the strength of will to fight it even when the odds of survival were next to nothing. That spirit, even if it doesn't seem to take probability or traditional threat assessment into account, what it sees is that to do nothing dooms us all with a remarkable certainty and that the true threat is not to act in the face of tyranny.

There were others, Scientists and Philosophers, truth seekers and truth speakers, they stood on the shoulders of giants and because of it saw great truth, even Einstein himself studied under Planck and they all gave us great ideas they might not have seen had others not laid the foundations for their discoveries. We all believe those who came before us were somehow greater than us, a nostalgia for the past, but standing upon the shoulders of giants is how we have built our civilization and no discovery is any less powerful simply because it took the work of others to achieve. If we cannot exceed the potential of men before us in our own eyes then how can we ever find ourselves worthy. To believe the best in behind us is simply to believe that it's all downhill from here, an attitude that by denying the possibility denies the opportunity for such things to happen, the day we stop believing in heroes is the day they cease to be and all it takes to bring them back and to bring back a world of legends walking like giants among men is for one foolish child to believe he can be one someday.

We have put men on the moon, we have split the atom, we have cured almost all of the diseases that killed our ancestors yet we cannot see that we are still worthy. We may not live in a world where it is a great and wise thing to say that illness is not caused by demons, but that is no longer something that makes us stupid, what makes us stupid is that in all we understand that we do not understand our contributions are still as great today as the contributions of men like Pythagoras, Plato and Hippocrates. In an ocean a drop of wisdom may seem like a drop but in a desert it will seem like an ocean.

Becoming a hero is the most difficult thing in the world, getting it right so that you won't leave a legacy of pain and misery is even more difficult. Buddha's compassion meaning correct action to yield correct results is not something that requires wisdom but in most cases requires the ability to predict the future. It is impossible to always act in a way that hurts no-one and makes everyone's lives better and good intentions can pave the way to hell. Being a true hero is more about luck than anything else and if your luck runs out you will likely become a monster in terms of how you are remembered. Che Guevara worked with lepers, he is remembered as a butcher who only helped to pave the way for Castro's Cuba. Being remembered as a hero is more difficult than acting like one and with history being written by the victors a hero like Guy Fawkes can become a memory of treason and terrorism, burned as an effigy more to remind us never to step out of line or risk torture, death and being burned for all eternity. Remember, remember the fifth of November, gunpowder, treason and plot. We tend to forget how bad things were in the early 17th century, but this was four hundred years ago and Britain was oppressed in such horrific ways. Yes he tried to blow up parliament but they weren't stupid and misguided cowardly little wretches like today, they were pure evil and exploiting people mostly for fun. Why do we say to remember if we are going to forget why he tried to do it. He failed, but not to do something evil, he failed to free his country and was brutally tortured for it along with everyone who tried to help him. He knew he faced torture, public execution and being branded a traitor for centuries but what he tried to do he did for us, for the future, so stop celebrating the fifth of November as the day a terrorist got what he got, don't burn an effigy, just solemnly remember that it's the day a group of sadistic bastards didn't get what they deserved, the day a group of fucking heroes failed to do something great, so remember that and, well.... set off some big fireworks, I'm pretty sure he'd appreciate us remembering him with explosives.

Heroes inspired me all my life, I couldn't give up no matter how bad things were because they wouldn't.

Heroes are often about refusing to look reality in the face and strangely enough as if reality likes their ideas better than what it is, reality changes to agree with them. I often think that's what we are all capable of being and what heroes are, so fantastically insane reality changes itself just to accommodate them. It was what I was determined to be and by the time I had grown up a bit my ideas had evolved a great deal.

The Green Jacket, the thing I had expected to evolve into, a symbol of courage and hope to bring light into the darkest time in human history, the apocalypse of our own creation. Unexpectedly I never did wind up becoming a hero, unexpectedly for me at least, but this was still the hero I wanted to become. I wanted to be a hero not so much for myself though there was a part of me that believed saving the world was the only thing I could do that would ever make anyone like me, mostly I just wanted to save the world for everyone else having almost given up on ever being happy myself. I was supposed to found the resistance, lead a revolution and bring the entire world into a new glorious age of enlightenment, so nothing too grand eh? These expectations gave me hope while everything else in my life was crap, as long as I could believe I was some kind of messiah and all the crap in my life merely tests then there was something to hold on to, the madness that kept me alive.

Chapter 3: The One

Okay, I know I was crazy and so should you since it's what the book is about, but I thought I was supposed to save the world, not a far leap from believing that you're someone who will. I thought, by the time I was thirteen that I was The One. I hadn't been able to put a name to it before, The Messiah had non-violent connotations not super-speed ass kicking connotations even if it was "The Second Coming and this time he's pissed!" So The One became my way of referring to it and I started looking for the woman whose love would set me free. I knew the truth, that it was all illusion. That would be the case for anything, computer simulated or otherwise. Our minds aren't capable of seeing what is, just a fraction of it and even then we process it into a radical misinterpretation of what it actually is, not a small spectrum of electromagnetic radiation reflected by the surface electrons of a collection of particles made almost completely of nothing, no we see a green leaf. It's not green, the surface electrons from one chemical in particular, the chlorophyll, are reflecting the light from our detectable spectrum that we interpret as green. What we see is not the truth, just our interpretation of it and this applies not only to sight but to perception itself.

These things I understood, and I interpreted them as I saw fit. If the world was illusion then of course we make reality in an unconscious way, the projector and the projection. This is also commonly understood in Buddhism in terms of, you are the Universe and everything in it. So I believed that if someone could on a conscious level tap into their ability to form the world and everything in it that they could not only change the world by changing themselves, but practically re-write or even just ignore the laws of physics, the history of the

Universe, our future, ourselves, everything. This is what I saw, that no matter what existence was we could change anything on any level, whether we knew it or not we were all as Gods. I didn't understand however that this was practically the little understood notion of Luciferianism. I had achieved what most of these people hadn't and in a more total understanding than them, I was perhaps Lucifer. Yes my messianic complex had essentially made me the anti-Christ, an irony that in itself was pretty damn funny. The man with all the answers is anti-Christ, the man who saves the world is anti-Christ and the man who denies God and believes himself God is the man of sin himself, the Anti-Christ.

I had actually become a witch, or warlock if you will, when I was indoctrinated into a coven of few years back. I'd been watching Buffy and I wanted superpowers, I knew I couldn't be a slayer but a witch seemed almost possible. So since I believed magic could actually be used for good, that it was mankind's only innate power and that despite what the church said about witches they were probably wrong and trying to eliminate pagans who knew what Easter and Christmas were supposed to be and therefore knew not only that the story of Jesus was a literal interpretation of the movements of the stars and the sun but that they actually had the nerve to just paste it over Pagan holidays. The sun reaching its lowest point when the northern cross intersects with it, the sun dying on the cross, and staying there for three days then rising again, yes it's the story of the resurrection, then the sun rises in the sky or heavens, it ascends into heaven. I know, I used to be Christian and it seemed unbelievable to me but there it is, this takes place at Christmas, the Death of Jesus star story takes place at the time we're supposed to believe he was born, this also is the origin of the story of the birth of Jesus. When the sun rises on the 25th of December, three stars those from Orion's belt actually align to point to the place of the sunrise on December 25th, these stars are known as the three kings. They also seem to follow the star in the east, the bright star Sirius. So the three kings followed the star in the east to find the birth of the sun. Weird.

So I became a witch, and while this may seem like one of those funny stories about the misunderstandings of youth people even today probably still fear witches. I wondered one day as the entirety of my English class began chanting "Burn him!" yelling and screaming like an angry mob if this weren't the case however they probably just didn't like me the way nobody does. Perhaps they somehow subconsciously were aware of those past centuries when morons murdered people based on superstition and misunderstanding or perhaps they merely hated me, I can't speculate as to what they were thinking. Most of the time demonic possession was nothing more than ergotism caused by eating grain containing fungus. In other words they acted like they were possessed because they were tripping on acid and people were killed for it. Hippocrates himself said that illness isn't caused by demons thousands of years before, nobody in Christendom got the memo it seems. So witch trials began and a witch trial is basically execution. If you survive being drowned, you're burned. The test by water. So if anyone accused you of being a witch you would be dead. "Oh I saw him doing dark magicks I did!" Was basically an excuse to have your neighbour killed. Had he committed murder he would have been killed, but accusing someone of being a witch is not something that comes back on you even if the witch is found innocent because they drowned. A way to have someone horrifically murdered without repercussions, something no good person would consider.

Modern equivalents do of course exist, things we fear so much even being innocent is not enough to protect you from being murdered for it, where one careless accusation from a horrendous bastard is enough to drive people to total hysteria. I'm sure you can think of several.

Witchcraft seemed to me to be a pathway to my ultimate goals, the power of a god and worldwide unity and yet there was so much division and misunderstanding that these things needed to be tackled too. I was determined to unite all of the religions based on their similarities, stop war by uniting all governments in a single world government and through understanding the nature of reality we would take our place as Gods among the stars. If it meant war to bring peace then so be it, I would allow no other to lead this world. I was kind of stupid. I hadn't actually read the book of Revelations yet but in the end once I had I decided that Christianity itself was lying, it wasn't a representation of God, just a few corrupt men trying to control the masses. I speculated that it was the means by which the Roman empire continued its dominance over the world after its public fall, by remaining in the shadows and by appearing publicly as champions of the people and justice and servants of truth and God. I was probably right but it's best not to push opinion and speculation as truth.

So there I was, a fulfillment of biblical prophecy, Lucifer of Luciferianism, the Anti-Christ of Christianity and God of all existence. How my messiah complex turned into a God complex I don't know, but there we are. The plan of course was world-wide domination and while I'm not sure how, my desire to become a hero the likes of which is unheard of outside fantasy novels and games had turned me into a villain of such desire and ambition the likes of which is unheard of outside of fantasy novels and games. Irony. I know this was all probably madness, probably, but it all seemed so real at the time, I was the Messiah, The Antichrist, God, the Devil and quite frankly this all made sense. The battle between Good and Evil, between light and darkness was not being waged in the Universe without but in the Universe within. In the choices of every person and the opportunity for corruption and evil, or redemption and compassion in every person, at every moment. I still believe the fate of the world is in the hands of every person, I just don't think it's all about me anymore, maybe I was the Devil and maybe I've changed. Who's to say?

If you know either way, how do you know, and how do you know you know? We trust in what we believe so strongly we call it knowledge but we know nothing and never can. All we can do is qualify what we believe. If I can trust the observations I have made and they are based upon the structure of unchanging rules then barring any unforeseen changes in these rules I can predict it's behaviour thus:

That is the supposition of all science, we determine the nature of things by observation based upon the assumption that observation is a viable means to do so and the assumption that anything can be said to be real. In other words Science is only true if nobody changes the rules and if anything can ever be said to be real meaning that while Science does not presuppose the existence of a god, it still presupposes the unproven existence of things and as such is not nearly as conclusive as I once believed. It is incredibly useful, saves billions of lives, it brings technology into our lives and makes the world an altogether more interesting place through it's almost unimaginable potential, it suggests remarkable things about ourselves and our Universe, we just don't know whether it's real or not. The thing about what I was imagining was that it couldn't be disproved by Science, Science is a remarkable network of equations, a matrix of programming but what I was suggesting was becoming the programmer, to go beyond the program and have a role in the constant changing of the Universe before it even gets to science, the program creating the simulation. Getting there before the world is formed was the idea, not in the sense of time but in the sense of something non-temporal and non-spacey, out in the midst of Universal existence, somewhere between the Void and form where I could stand, in that place between existence and nothingness and make spectacular things happen. I believed it could be achieved and perhaps saw more than most, to stand in that place most dare not look, perhaps I do perhaps I don't, I wouldn't tell you even if I knew.

Weird things seem to happen to me all the time now, like an unseen self constantly trying to tell me, Here I Am! I can be thinking something and have the same words appear in the world, on sign posts, on the radio or on television. Sometimes I'm playing on a computer game and watching television at the same time when on the television, in my head and on the computer game the same words appear, assumption, memory, predictable TV and of course coincidence are all possible and more likely reasons. This was of course coincidence, two or more of the same thing co-existing at the moment of incidence, however just because something is coincidence doesn't mean that it means nothing.

These ways of thinking sent me completely insane. When you dismiss rational thoughts the inevitable result is irrational ones.

Whether or not I was right or it was real I can't say, many people say they're right and say something is real because they never properly evaluate whether it is or not. Nothing can ever be said to be real and half the time I don't know whether I'm right about anything. This could be the dream of the Cosmic Space Weasel of Antaris 5, and the cosmic space weasel itself might just be something I imagined which itself is imagining me. Simultaneous co-creation I call it, the relationship between two unreal things as they create each others existence. Neither one is real of course, not as we would define it, but the dream dreaming the dreamer that dreams the dreamer dreaming the dream could be all anything ever is and we could never ever know one way or the other. A simulated person acts like it exists, it acts like it believes it exists, yet believes nothing, never acts and in fact doesn't exist. A simulated person might think they exist and might even think they think but only do so because they're programmed to, I might only believe differently and question it because I'm programmed to do that. So here we are knowing nothing except that we think we know things completely at the mercy of our own imaginations and curious natures when the only definable truth is that if there is anything, even just a dream, something exists no matter how far removed we are from it. In Buddhism this is the Void.

I know I keep going on about non-things that never happened but this is how I thought. Half my life or more wasn't events that 'happened' but thoughts that I thought. Most people say I think too much, I would say they don't think enough, but then 'we' are always the standard against which 'we' judge everything else. I spent more than half my life in my head and in my head things happen much faster than in the world. People look at me and think I'm 23, they talk to me and are often confused by the fact that I talk like I'm thousands of years old, born in the distant past and from the future, but I have lived more in these few years than most people ever get to and I'll be thousands of years older before I die. I have seen cultures and civilizations rise and fall, I have met heroes and villains, angels and demons, I have lived the future and the past because I have something that makes me live forever wherever I wish to live, I have an imagination.

Chapter 4: Human Nature

In the search for answers if someone were to create a device capable of determining the nature of reality it would only be able to do so in relation to itself. Before being able to give you an answer it would first have to ask, "Am I real?" Some have speculated that this was the initial blueprint for design of humans, however we have only progressed as far as knowing, "This world may not be real but this report still has to be in by Friday."

Notre Dame was actually the name of another school in Sheffield, not my school but knowing a hunchbacked freak like myself lived near a place called Notre Dame frequently gave me pause to think. It was not a normal hunch, not the genetic hunch from a spinal defect, just the kind of thing that happens when your spirit breaks and you no longer hold your head high or even have the strength to align your spine properly. Needless to say, people noticed and when insecure, suffering people see the one person more hurt and insecure than themselves all they see is a chance to take out their misery on someone else without fear of retaliation or repercussions. I guess it's just nature's way of telling you not to bother anymore, when you're already feeling as bad as you think you can and everyone seems intent on going out of their way to make you feel worse, nature's way of telling you to lose at life gracefully and throw yourself off a nice tall bridge. This was not an option I liked, things might get better eventually if you kept going, but dying was somewhat an end to that possibility just to prevent the inevitability of further suffering. But my ancestry was not the sort of thing that would let me give up on my life just because it was cold, miserable, violent and constantly being attacked by the

English.

I come from Scottish ancestry which would explain why I'm 6'4" with a scowl that could frighten wild dogs but I'm also one of the only people in the world who can be almost certain that they're of Viking descent. Sure people from Norway can say they descend from Viking ancestry, but only the cowards too scared to ride across a hundred miles of freezing ocean on a three metre long plank of wood to go face innumerable hordes. Those raping, pillaging inhuman monsters are where I descend from. It's well known they stopped halfway between Norway and Scotland at the Shetland isles and it's well known what they did when they got there and after a thousand or more years of history practically everyone from Shetland is in some way descended from Viking warriors. I'm probably making a lot of this up but everyone in Shetland speaks English with a Norwegian accent which makes my idea of history look all the sweeter now doesn't it?

It made a lot of sense to me that in a world where I couldn't carry a sword or kill someone for the crime of disrespecting me that I would have to struggle with my nature but then human nature as we define it is not how humans naturally behave and as such in order to act like responsible people, we all must struggle with our natures. I think it was this most of all that made me hate those who didn't struggle with their natures. They seemed to be under the impression that I was somehow naturally a good person, they were naturally the way they were, competitive and violent but they didn't seem to grasp that we're all competitive and violent, we're all animals and capable of beastly things, the only difference between us was that I resisted and overcame my nature while they never saw that this was what everyone was required to do, by law, by civilization and by conscience.

Our civilization and the way we think about things is rather stupid, especially among those who would call themselves intelligent. Intelligent people think, as I once did, that there is some great natural difference between all people that makes some people stupider than others. Firstly, those people we often associate with stupidity are in fact in possession of one of the most sophisticated pieces of hardware on the planet, a human brain. We must try to remember this, secondly, most people who grow up achieving little have also grown up in emotional circumstances, angry people are using their limbic system more and their left pre-frontal cortex less. As one increases the other decreases, hence why we become less rational when angry and less angry when we rationalize it. To use your rationality properly is a skill and one that becomes increasingly difficult to learn as we get older, however when the limbic system is used more often it too can become dominant, meaning you are more likely to react emotionally than rationally. More likely to react violently than consider things calmly. The fact is that there are learning disabilities as well as people who learn faster but I personally learned quickly because of associative memory which was a technique I learned.

Most people would consider me very clever, but like most of the things I know, this thing which I became is something I trained myself to be. The same is true of so called stupid people, they are not stupid or evil, they are angry and they have learned to allow their limbic system to be their controlling influence diminishing the effect their rational brain has on their actions. Rationally speaking, murder is not only wrong but rather foolish, people who commit murder, 'in the heat of the moment' would never do so normally, they only do so because their limbic system, their anger, is telling them to kill but their rational side simply does not engage. Rationally most people would never commit murder but we are all animals and self-defense from perceived threats is a powerful natural instinct, one which can completely override a more rational approach to self-preservation leading almost any person to kill. We are all killers, we tell ourselves we're not because we find these things horrific and don't want to admit it, but we're all far too capable of murder because in genetics we are only a verbal reasoning center away from creatures with no inhibitions about killing.

Anyway, if you're stupid enough to believe good genes made you clever and bad genes made others stupid, bear in mind that everyone is capable of understanding our most advanced scientific discoveries, we simply fail them because we assume they'll never learn. Even if you do have a genetic advantage in intellect, this surely requires of you to use that intellect not only to find the truth but to act accordingly. We all have human brains and while I don't wish to dispute that intelligence may be a factor, I believe that larger factors must be at work because there is no possibility something as sophisticated and powerful as a human mind can be stupid. Memory techniques can be learned, rationality can be diminished by use of the limbic system and IQ test scores can increase a great deal if you study for them. These are facts, intelligence is speculation.

Saying a human brain is stupid is like saying a supercomputer is poorly designed because the problem can't be with Windows 95. Point well-made I do believe. Supercomputers cannot reach their full potential without equally sophisticated programming, we have not even begun to imagine what our minds are capable of, not memorizing the phone book in minutes, not calculating Pi to a thousand decimal places in your head, our minds are capable of far greater things than we even know yet.

This is our real problem, where the system fails not only these people but the people who want to learn but cannot because those who don't want to learn won't let them and the greatest arrogance of our age is to think we have even come close to a system that works.

Chapter 5: Drugs, Rock and Roll and Imposed Celibacy

My celibacy was never a life choice, it was somewhat imposed in fact despite efforts on my part to correct this. I never had that first love or teenage romance people talk about as being the best time of their life, well not with a woman anyway. My first love was Mary Jane.

She smelled so great, she tasted so good and she made me feel like no woman could, so fucking high. It was a marriage made in heaven, I had problems, social problems, love life problems, I was twisted and homicidal from years of constant bullying not to mention horrifically traumatized and crazy because of some other horrific shit and she made me forget and not care. I couldn't drink, I mean I knew where to buy it from but shortly after my first trauma incident when I was still in complete denial about having PTSD I bought a litre bottle of vodka and drank it all. I was sick for three days and I almost died, from then on I realised I would probably die if I tried drinking away my problems. Then I heard the most remarkable thing, Weed won't kill you, you can't OD. You can whitey if you smoke too much but it won't kill you. To me it was still part of those 'Drugs', the indiscriminate label meant to discriminate against every illegal substance as bad and dangerous and going to kill you and destroy your life, so it wasn't exactly something I'd consider at first but my mates as I discovered were all stoners. Even my brother had been smoking weed and I had never even seen that all of this was going on right under my nose. Still, it was a big, glaring line to cross and I did so hesitantly. My first time trying it, I didn't inhale. Dave had invited me up to his house for a sesh since I said I'd like to try it, so I cycled up not wanting my Mum to drop me off to go do drugs. I felt enough like I was betraying her trust without getting her to enable me. Since I was hesitant about it Dave showed me pictures he'd taken of him smoking weed with a few people, it was actually quite scary because they all seemed so pale, their faces were so happy and full of life yet their bodies seemed to disagree with what their faces were telling me.

Having seen this 'evidence' meant to abate my fears it felt like a confirmation of my inhibitions about drugs stealing you soul, I played along for a bit but in the end I was too scared, I just wanted to walk up to the edge and look over but not actually take the plunge. As Dave continued to get more high with his friend I felt like the prude at the party as it turned into an orgy, looking for the nearest exit and trying to make a dash without being impolite. Giggling behind me as I hopped on my bike and rode downhill, I thought to myself, "I never have any fun." The moment I arrived home I told my Mum everything, I was afraid she'd smell the weed on my hoody and know I'd been doing drugs. Having betrayed her trust once I didn't want to lie to her as well, I told her everything and she made me promise never to visit Dave's house again. I was back there next week.

I was still captivated by the idea of something that can make you happy, I was rarely happy and often miserable, my life was practically hell. I was constantly bullied by people who hurt me because they thought I was rich, because they thought that I must believe I was better than them just because I was smart. Still they had no idea I had grown up poor on a road where smack addicts dumped their used syringes in our garden, raised by a single mother, missed birthday presents, few friends, constantly bullied by people who turned it into an art form managing to destroy what little self-esteem I had left, no girlfriends or sex life just the constant sexual frustration wearing me down and of course haunted by something that would haunt them if I so much as told them what had happened and all this by the time I was sixteen. I had two options, to continue to hold on to the hope that in three years I'd be at Uni and three years later I'd be a respected scientist in the field of something, or face the fact that I'd be dead in less than a year hanged with slit wrists and throat having nailed a sign to my chest saying "Are you happy now fuckheads?"

I caved, I had begged my mother to let me see a therapist since I was fourteen but she never wanted to believe her son was in so much pain and I can't fault her for that, but in the absence of psychiatric help from a professional and the help of strong medication I had to self-medicate just to keep myself going. My real first spliff was quite a nice one, I met up with Dave and the other three members of the Awesome Foursome, Liam, Jack and the other Dave. We all put in, that's where you have a communal money pile and you convert it into a communal ganja pile and we went off to see the wizard, chasing dragons. I had always been into fantasy games but I had no idea just how magical life could be, I put about five quids worth of weed into my first spliff and smoked it all myself as we all did that day. We sat in a quiet forest clearing which isn't that uncommon in Sheffield and smoked our little spiffs. I didn't even need someone to tell when to stop before I whitey, I just stopped when I forgot that I was even smoking and just stared at the trees. I could feel it, I could smell it, the trees were alive, this we all know but at the time it seemed like such a revelation, they were buzzing and glowing and alive. For the first time in my life the world seemed to come into full colour, rather than the painful march towards death it had always been and I felt such joy just to be one of the few lucky people that gets to exist at all. Such noble thoughts had never come to me before, no appreciation just to exist or joy at life's simplest wonders, it had all been rage and hate and fear and pain, then suddenly, there was light.

The time spent in the woods didn't last much longer before someone suggested the single greatest idea I had ever heard, "Let's go to the chippy." Brilliant I thought, utter simplicity yet such genius, there truly is nothing I want more right now than some food but, how did you know? This was when I learned of the munchies, a shared experience by stoners in the true appreciation of food. No connoisseur or aficionado of the food world has ever felt such delight as a stoner having his first enormous meal on the munchies. Oily chips and battered sausage, for some reason things always taste better when battered, it was heaven, every bite of it and every moment of appreciation knowing your stomach was comfortably stuffed. It was heaven.

The Awesome Foursome and the Fifth Wheel never really became a thing, in fact after we all split up to meander back home and collapse we never met up like that again, I know the Awesome Foursome went on many previous adventures and had a great many missions to go but I never found a place among them, perhaps because there were already four.

My next goal of course was to make sure I always had the ability to smoke weed and despite having seen the final result wanted to make certain I had everything needed. Dave explained the necessities to me, tobacco, papers, roach paper, a lighter and of course the cannabis. Tobacco and papers were readily available to a sixteen year old at the time as were lighters. Roach paper I found at the nearby paraphernalia shop as well as a tinny to hold it all in. I almost felt complete in my transition to stoner lifestyle after all if the police were to search me and find it that's exactly what they'd assume I was, I would however be uncharged, not even given a warning because I still lacked that essential component of both the lifestyle and the mindset, Ganja. I had no contacts, no dealers, no nothing, which meant no Ganja. The only person I knew of who might be willing to help was Dave and things did not go well.

I asked if he could help maybe give me the number of one of his dealers but of course he said no, I asked him if he could pick me up some, he asked why, I said to hold onto some in case I wanted to smoke, he said no. I had neglected to realise that all evidence to the contrary these were not care-free people, you couldn't even call them careless. Despite cannabis not being fiercely policed and it being downgraded to a class C drug, these were meticulously cautious people who didn't get caught. Holding on to weed was rare, and if they picked up they would probably smoke it all right then. They didn't spread contacts around or even talk about it too much. Names, numbers and addresses were closely guarded secrets and a good contact was a sign of strength or dominance among people who must rely on them to score. As a student of the human condition and science in general I found this to be fascinating from an anthropological perspective, a true sub-culture subsisting in a hostile environment by means of cautious behaviour that defies an outsider's views on expected behaviour. Playing the discriminatory misunderstanding of cannabis culture against them in order to thrive. Those who most oppose them are least able to understand, predict or challenge their behavior, not only a brilliant strategy but one which apparently was not derived from a full understanding of this, simply awareness of danger and response.

In many ways I found this to be an intriguing idea even if my knowledge was limited and my assumptions were many, still intrigue had never been enough to keep the wolf from the door before and as such I was still faced with the pressing issue of picking up again before the horror of my life became too obvious again. Often tackling a problem in a straightforward manner proves unsuccessful, I found the answer to my problem was not to seek a remedy from the expected source, the tree already known to give fruit but by checking a tree I could expect but not know to be more "fruitful". Brothers often drift apart as they get older, even when they are still living under the same roof. This was true of my family too. My brothers had made my life more difficult, even when I had a chance to escape the bullying at school, it still continued at home. When staying with my dad for a weekend he was always the propagator and my brothers would join in for the insults and the laughter, when at home with my mum it was always my older brother Adrian who kept the fear mounting. Not only were there always threats of physical violence if I went into his room, he just thought I did, a toy was missing even though he might have misplaced it or it could've been Brian, anything at all went wrong in his life at any point or if he just felt like it, there were also the constant insults and the laughter at my expense around the dinner table every night. But Brian while we had grown apart was close to my own age and we had always been closer than either of us were with Adrian. By this time Brian had his own life, his own friends and since we went to different schools they weren't even people I'd ever met, but when I did I was glad to know them.

Some of the smartest people I've ever known and kinder people than I had ever hoped to meet were stoners. Then again this was just the means by which I met them, I'm sure there are people who smoke weed who also happen to find a lot of fun with only two items in their possession, like a live dog and a sharp knife for instance, or a wild bird and an electrified cage. Smoking weed does not make you a good person, it can make you calm, hyper, happy, sad, forgetful, crazy, crazy, crazy or even crazy but karmically speaking, were this a Good/Evil open choice computer game you would be unaffected in your alignment, unless it was made by those 'war on drugs' people in which case you'd probably turn to completely evil, grow horns and worship Satan in those few seconds before it kills you instantly.

My brother was a stoner and in a weird way walking in on someone trying to hide smoking weed from you is like walking in on someone masturbating, those few frantic seconds while they try to hide what they're doing. Fortunately since he wasn't masturbating I could calmly walk into the room instead of anxiously walking out and then dreading looking him in the face ever again. I told him that I was a stoner too, I wasn't really by this point, just a poser but I do pose well, like a Brazilian model. We chatted for a bit, smoked a bit of weed but it didn't snag until later that since we were both stoners the only people in the house we didn't have to hide this from was each other. It was a nice experience, finding acceptance in my own home when I think we both felt ashamed. This was a betrayal of our mother's trust but as long as we had each other's acceptance and a large pile of Ganj we could feel good about it. This I think was the beginning of a beautiful friendship, several in fact.

Ollie was brilliant, intellectually brilliant enough to make me look like an idiot sometimes, clever enough in fact that he quit smoking weed before I even started. This did make him a bit of an outsider but he never caved to peer pressure and I'm actually pretty proud to know someone with that strength of will. Cam was pretty nasty to me at first, like a cat who's not quite sure whether the new cat in the house is supposed to be there or just a stray that's wandered into his home without anyone else noticing. He was hippie born and hippie raised, his mother was a folk singer and his father was an art teacher, there's probably a Monty python joke in there somewhere. He was the closest person to famous I'd ever met, which made him pretty cool in my book, after all this wasn't cheap Hollywood famous, this was low-down gritty folk music famous.

Naz, well he's the hardest to describe, despite the fact that I'm telling you almost nothing about all of them, but Naz was the coolest person anybody can ever have the hope of meeting. No leather jackets or sunglasses, he's not the Fonz or anything, y'know, he's not a jackass. He'd probably instead be walking down the road in a dressing gown except he would never be concerned by the stares he was getting. He's very protective of the mocha skinned goddesses he calls sisters and he sleeps with a Persian battle axe above his bed. Rob, most likely to pull. The guy had a full beard when he was thirteen and people just seem to love him, especially female people, especially the ones I fancy. I was pretty jealous of him at times but he was a good guy and a good friend and my god the man deserves some props for those skills of his. Greg, the guy had almost the skills of Rob but if you wanted to test your philosophy he was the one to talk to. If there were holes, he would find them and readily point out your mistakes if you were ever foolhardy enough to believe you might actually have figured out something important. Greg was a great guy, he kept me on my toes and kept me thinking sane for a long time. Without him I would have succumbed to my juvenile fantasies about single-handedly saving the world with superpowers and ten years down the line with no life and still no superpowers I'd probably have killed myself.

The aforementioned Dave was the best friend I'd ever had and I still feel he is even now. He was true blue but when I met him he was a very different guy. He was convinced despite being one of the smartest people I've ever met that he wasn't all that bright. As a boffin, an authority on cleverness I reassured him that anyone who can follow a conversation with me completely without going insane or beginning to hear white noise halfway through is most assuredly clever. Dave of course could always keep up with me and was always half the conversation or more. I never liked to feel superior around people, it made me feel guilty and evil which in a strange way actually made me feel inferior. Still with friends it's nice not have the inferiority complex about your superiority complex, it can make things so complex.

Life was looking up for the first time ever, I had good friends and plenty of them and with a little help from my friends I had a steady supply of green. We all shared and those of us with more shared more and in a weird way using only one resource we had created an egalitarian, resource based cooperative. We had our own little society and it was free from the problems everyone else faced, there was no bigotry or hatred, no poverty and very little crime. There was the occasional curiously misplaced joint but then every society has its problems. Regardless though we were happy as we were, we had friendship, we had drugs and we had music.

The music was the best part of those early years, that and the drugs. None of us had girlfriends except for Rob who balanced the scales by always having girlfriends, but we had music man. Muse's new album had come out and we were all still listening to Radiohead's past and bygone albums that still seemed to be ahead of the times years later. There was Bob Dylan, Martin Simpson and some good old blues. When tripping a bit on some good weed we all got into a bit of Lemon Jelly or Nightmares on Wax, because nothing's better for a good chill than some great chill out, but the air was sort of warm and a bit too humid with anticipation because GCSE's were over, summer had struck, we were out of school and something big was coming.

It wasn't sex of course, as I write this now I'm still a virgin, I was on a sort of society imposed celibacy thing back then. I would never choose to be celibate but when you're almost universally hated anyone who dated you would have to either already be a total outcast it therefore being impossible for things to be worse or just crazy enough to commit social suicide, but all the sixteen year old outcasts and suicide chicks were dating men in their thirties so I was out of luck. Still it was better than sex, well almost probably better than sex, I mean if you've never had sex and have no chance of having sex it was probably the sort of thing you could almost completely convince yourself was going to be better than sex, or at least you would probably exaggerate by describing it as better than sex. But still if I'd been waiting in line to get the new Radiohead album and an eighteen year old Goth chick said, "If you never buy this album you can fuck me." I think we all know where the chips would fall. Still no Goth chick, no fucking, just one fucking good or at least wankingly good Radiohead album. There There, while unbelievably high sitting in a Botanical Garden at night. I don't think I need say anymore.

The girlfriend thing was kind of an issue for me because I didn't really have any other options. I was sixteen so fucking guys was out, and plus an openly gay or even bisexual person in Yorkshire is something not heard of in schools. In the workplace maybe, but in public schools in Yorkshire the word gay despite originally being a word originally meaning happy was actually a euphemism for bad. People really do still wonder why the suicide rate is so high among gay teens, I mean are they stupid or something? Not only is all this talk allowed even though it reinforces the idea that being gay is bad but by the time you're old enough to understand these things, which for me was about fourteen, you realise gay people are openly discriminated against by law as well. I mean you can go to Canada and get married but not on British soil of course. The fact is there is only one reason to stop gay people getting married, if you don't like gays and think they're less than people therefore they can't get married like real people. Surely any two people in love deserve to have their love sanctified by whatever God or gods or spirits or nether lichs they believe in regardless of gender or lack thereof. Still what can you expect, there are still people in government trying to take rights from gays but what else can they take besides our dignity as equal human beings. There's at least one politician I can think of who's openly against rights for gays and if there's one gay-intolerant politician you're seeing there's probably a whole lot more you aren't seeing.

So if the girlfriend thing was out and so was the guy thing then there was only porn, hollow, painful porn, the thing that reminds you you're single and lonely and leaves you feeling fucked in a bad way. Porn is a sick mistress, she has her whips, her gag-balls, handcuffs, fake tits, blown o-rings, masks, diseases and serious drug issues, but if you slip her a dollar she'll dance for you. It's sad when you've spent your life trying to be a good person and then you find yourself in a questionably moral situation. I thought the sex thing would sort itself out, that I'd find love, instead I wound up alone and miserable looking at graphic images of beautiful young women, probably about as lost and alone as I was yet I was the one exploiting them. I might as well have been the one misleading them into exploitation if I was going to reap the benefits of it. To me sex was always supposed to be about love, but this... There was no love, not even a sign that they were enjoying themselves, just this fake venire of actual emotion from the least skilled actors the world has ever seen. "Oh baby give it to me!" is about as convincing as a person sitting on a bicycle making a motorcycle engine noise trying to make you jealous of his new Harley. Anyone with any concept of reality can tell when someone's trying to deceive the eyes with an unconvincing sound. Hollow, hollow porn. I dreamt of finding true love, of a beautiful romance, stolen moments in inappropriate places and tender embraces in the bedroom. Porn satisfies roughly zero percent of that need, it's little more than a tool to achieve ejaculation when you thoroughly believe no-one will ever love you, because at least you can still pay for some hollow and unsatisfying sex from a woman you barely know. That's all porn is really, prostitution at a distance with less than half the fun, and twice the feel of being in a cheap motel.

The summer was actually the best time of my life, most of the time I was out of the house. Smoking weed in the park, smoking weed on a hill, smoking weed in a disused shed, it was great partly because of all the smoking weed. At first weed is great fun, like pouring a rainbow and sound byte native American and Chinese wisdom into your head. Sometimes it can feel like the greatest journey of discovery of your life and for me it was when I first saw it. A hero, wearing his Green Jacket that draped like a cloak, the dual symbolism of magic and military. As old as time itself yet each time he's born again he can remember almost nothing, stuck in a single life, a single loop as time repeats itself over and over again for each time he struggles and fights to stop the apocalypse and each time fails, never achieving his true potential, yet as the world burns this lonely soul uses the last of his strength to travel back and try again with nothing but faint memories to guide him to victory. Originally one of a pair, a pair of lovers. The first to find true love, yet married as they were, their union was cursed by his wife before they were murdered by her lover. Doomed never to touch again, never to know each other's embrace, only to live forever and forever apart. Broken as the ritual was by a vicious and bloody murder the lovers were doomed not to eternity in one life but to return over and over, to reincarnate and forget past mistakes. The witch reveled in her victory, greater than she had wished, for without memory of past mistakes one cannot break the spell with one tender kiss. The kiss thing is classic fairy tale I thought, as is the witch and the brutal murder. It was a magical moment for me and I felt like I was seeing the hero I could be. A near invincible, magic-wielding, gun-toting maniac on a mission to save the world. Sadly things did not pan out so magically. I wound up an emotionally vulnerable laptop wielding maniac on a mission to write a story about a near invincible, magic-wielding, gun-toting maniac on a mission to save the world. Still, good times in bon temps.

Most of my time smoking weed was spent in my head, it seemed logical to me for where else can you best appreciate something that is affecting your head, however while that summer was great this much I know, as drugs like weed and alcohol go, the better the night the less you remember, and this was a great summer. The things I remember best were the best times and the worst times, the best of which were the times spent listening to music while smoking spliffs the worst times were terrible.

We had been listening to music in the Botanics, some good old fashioned Radiohead's latest album. As it was night it involved a little climbing and jumping in order to get in and out of the Botanics, a far cry from breaking and entering. We were climbing back over the wall when suddenly I felt overcome by a strange feeling. As I hit the ground on the other side I found myself unable to catch my fall or even stand back up. Rushing up to me Dave worried I had become dizzy and hurt myself but for reasons I couldn't explain standing up was impossible. It felt terrible, not like a whitey which is just dizzying hallucinations and nausea, this was emptiness, meaninglessness. It was like seeing for absolutely certain that life, the universe and everything was meaningless and though I could not put words to it my body knew what it meant. There was no fight, no life, no impulse strong enough to tell me to get up. My mind had seen and my body had reacted and then the song came into my head, Just by Radiohead, the music video where a man is lying on the road but can't get up, the man whose words could cause the world to fall to its knees, the thing people just don't want to know. As the song grew louder it was like seeing the parallels of reality reflecting me, like seeing the world reflecting me, or me reflecting it, or both and neither. It was remarkable and terrible and until Dave told me to get up I couldn't, then the whole thing began to fade, like a bad dream and I stood up. With this thing I did what I always do, I put it into a box in a locked room, I tried to forget and I ran.

Chapter 6: A Brand New Freak

When the summer was up and I was returning to school I felt like a new man, I mean I still felt like a freak, but a new freak, a brand new freak. It was sixth form, A-levels and pretty much all the people who had tried to systematically murder my soul were gone. It was a new dawn, a new day and a new life for me, and I was feeling good.

Further Maths was pretty fun, there were only seven of us in the entire class and it was real maths, oh yes it was the good stuff. Mechanics, permutations and combinations, binomial expansion, beautiful maths that actually did stuff. Stuff you could use. Plus in a group of seven there was almost nobody who hated me, only six to be precise, and in further maths there is absolutely no-one who doesn't want to be there. Just pure unadulterated learning, and sweet lady maths is a delicate flower and a sexy tutor with glasses and the kind of pout that disappeared with the fifties. And now it was time to unravel her mysteries and get intimate with her delicates. I tried really hard to stick at it, but things get harder when you can't remember what happened last week. I mean it's one thing to learn when every morning for breakfast you have a spliff and one at lunchtime, but it's another thing entirely to remember it a week later. The work went from maths I could do in my sleep and a two hour exam I could finish in thirty minutes and still get an A+ at GCSE, to a 15 hour workload a week of much more difficult maths after severely lowering my IQ with constant self-doping, and going from perfect memory to forgetting whether I'd had my lunch yet with a half-eaten sausage sandwich still in my hands. I was fucked. I should've taken art, that drugs would've helped with, but advanced level mathematics, I might as well have been drunk. Though that was an idea I didn't pick up until a couple years later at Hillsborough.

I had gone from top of the pack to a salt-water fish five miles from the nearest body of ocean. I was completely fucked. My entire life had been nothing but dreaming of the day I'd escape from this monotonous shithole and finally be able to use my brain for something other than solving obvious questions and writing on paper destined only to be burned. I had one dream, that was it, a life beyond being a nobody treated like shit, a job where I could ruin other people's lives for a change, or make them better I was going to figure out whether it was scientific advancement or advanced scientific weaponry at university, and I had fucked up everything. Even to this day I am filled with a quiet rage whenever I see pictures of people I once knew having graduated from University. I should feel good for them, but being seven years behind is somewhat infuriating when everyone else isn't just because they didn't go insane. See that's the big reward folks, you overcome everything, you crawl out of the abyss, you climb the treacherous cliffs of madness and your final reward is being years behind everyone else with nothing to show for it but the answer "You don't want to know." whenever they ask you what you've been up to. Not to mention everyone thinks you're crazy.

Things were bad already and after a summer of general bliss and occasional madness I was learning quick solutions to difficult problems are usually bigger problems. I had traded in a bright future it seemed and those bullies who sought to deny me that had finally won. I was far too broken to be fixed and I knew it. The year went by quickly, I'd spend most of my time away from school though, leaving whenever I could just to escape what I knew would just be further disappointment. It's a hard thing to fight the inevitable, to keep turning up at school knowing you can't win. There were opportunities to socialize but of course no love life, still. I made new friends and we smoked some weed, we ate sausage sandwiches and I slowly gave up. My grades were slipping and I was growing more depressed. The weed wasn't doing its job but I couldn't do without either, just stuck in an ever downward moving spiral.

The year passed by like a strange nightmare you keep trying to snap out of while things keep getting worse, my teachers were upset, even dismayed by my current attendance and attitude. One of their best pupils had turned into nothing but a drug fueled husk. Uncommunicative, distant, anti-social the three bywords for trouble in the teacher's dictionary, yet there was nothing anyone could do as I was a long way from ever coming back. I'm sad to say my best memory from that year was some really good weed. I went to my friend Rick who'd been bragging about the strength of the Ganj he was smoking. This is pretty typical among stoners, not matter how shit the shit, the dealer will always tell you it's the shit. What wasn't typical was that this was crazy strong, the strongest shit I ever smoked, that it was more than just talk and this stuff actually did what it said on the tin, I mean on the tin it said, 'I like the pope, the pope smokes dope.' But I meant metaphorically, the stuff met up to the promised standard.

Nick delivered it to me at school, half an ounce of incredibly strong shit, however Nick in all his kindness had tried to increase my reputation among my peers by spreading the news around. This did not go well. He meant well but all this meant was that the meanest bastards in the school now knew I was carrying half an ounce of strong shit. A mean Somalian guy with a knife by the name of Asad and a group of punks small enough to be elves but crazy enough to carry knives were planning to ambush me. This was the day I learnt the true meaning of compassion. People who had hated me, been cruel to me in the past had passed a message along. I heard it through the grapevine, so to speak and asked Dave to back me up and hide the Ganj in his bag. When Asad and his Keebler elves ambushed me I already had my backstory covered. I took it home at break time, it's gone. After he pulled a knife I unleashed my kung Fu skills and aptly defeated him and his Wu Shu master. No, in fact there was mention of a knife but he never took it out and I have no desire to fight, nor to learn how to punch stuff no matter how much I respect the history, technique, mysticism and health benefits of Kung Fu.

He bought the story and I didn't meet him again for a while, but in the mean time I had some dope. This shit was awesome, it was like smoking crack laced with ket, you felt great but almost completely unaware of anything for about three hours. I hate daytime TV, but staring mindlessly without any awareness whatsoever at Trisha for three hours was the only time I ever enjoyed watching daytime TV, seeing it the way it's meant to be seen, without thinking once. I couldn't smoke this shit far from home though, after about half a spliff you were basically unconscious for three hours and well, even after you sobered up a long sit down was advisable. After about two spliffs I don't remember what happened to the rest, or about a week of my life, but after it was over I was feeling much better.

I tried my best for the rest of the year but, there was no last minute turn around, I didn't magically quit weed and live happily ever after, I failed, I flunked, I fucked up. F's across the board. I had two choices, admit failure and spend the rest of my life and my sanity chasing a dragon or quit weed, repeat the year and do better this time. I tried to find a middle ground, keep smoking weed and don't admit failure. Repeating the year made things easier, I'd learnt it all once so I just had to fill in the gaps. I still had to avoid Asad who kept threatening me for weed and bringing gigantic black guys to look for me. Ordinarily I'm quite eager to meet gigantic black guys but not when they're trying to kill me. So between avoiding the most dangerous bullies I'd ever had to deal with and trying to complete an A-level course while completely caned, I had a pretty rough year. But the toughest year of my life was just beginning and by the end I'd wish for death.

Chapter 7: A Long Time Coming

You can't fill a gap left by constant verbal and emotional abuse, a gap left by longing for the love of a woman, a gap left by unspeakable horrors that tear right through you, you can't fill a gap with drugs. Had I more help when I needed it most or simply less abuse it would never have come to this but as it was weed was not enough anymore. When my mum found out about me smoking weed or more correctly when I confessed she warned me that it's a gateway drug, so named because once the weed isn't enough anymore you turn to harder substances. I never wanted her to be right in that regard, I wanted weed to be safe and harmless even though I already knew it had ruined my life, but in the end for me at least I caved and it became time to try something harder. I wanted weed plus, stronger than the strongest weed and the best I could find were magic mushrooms. I knew the rumors about people who never come back, who lose their minds and can never be helped, and I also knew the stories of heroes who face great trials only to finally achieve the power they had been searching for and figured that would be me. Cool.

I was such a bloody fool it defies belief. Even writing about it now I just want to change what happens next as I spent so much time wishing I could do, but writing something different now doesn't change what happened it just means I don't have to remember. I tried them twice before actually, once nothing happened, too small a dose, the second time I tripped and it was painful and scary, the third time was the worst. I remember that feeling where reality begins to slip away, the wrong thought at that time can fuck you up for life, the second time I had a hair in mouth that despite removing it the first time kept trying to remove it for several hours before closing my eyes and listening to music, the third time I reflected.

To reflect when you have that capacity is insane, to think 'Am I me looking at you or am I you looking at me?' before the trip really kicks in well if you try it now you are insane or at least soon going to be. It was a nightmare, it was hell. Like having half the Universe trying to fit into your brain, like seeing God and knowing madness, like going to hell and seeing to fearsome face of the devil, certain bygone Christian beliefs were acting as means for the trip to manifest. But it wasn't the things I don't believe in that terrified me, it was the things I couldn't deny were true. Most people think you can't have coherent thoughts on a drug like psilocybin, you can. You just have to hope you don't.

The terror kept on mounting as I plunged away from reality fearing never to return, I was on the bad trip and I knew it. The things I saw of such indescribable horror were meant for me alone, it was my own personal hell crafted by my own mind. Everything I feared most became reality as my hopes and everything I call upon for strength turned against me, mutating into something fearful itself. Meaning, that pillar of my life was torn from me as I saw and beheld that there is no meaning and there never can be, no civilization lasts forever, it will disappear into the dust and be forgotten, how can it matter? Even if they could last forever what would that accomplish? There are no goals, no gains to this game only rules and eventually a civilization with nothing to learn and nothing to accomplish will die whether in spirit or in actual death, nothing is forever, nothing matters. Then I saw something more terrible than meaninglessness and the fragile impermanence of our existence. I saw eternity.

Nothing I had ever seen had been so frightening a

prospect, impermanence was terrible but eternity is almost worse. It has no beginning, it has no end but neither is it the snake swallowing it's tail. It just stretches out beyond sight or belief and what's more it has no meaning. There is no point to eternity, no point to existence, no point to anything. This isn't glorious, it isn't even creation it's a twisted joke it's best not to look too closely at. It's all that can ever be, there are only two bad choices. That is not what existence was supposed to be. Then I saw again a face, the face of a man whom I know understood all too well. The point of this place was for God to forget. Eternity was unbearable, to be completely alone, to be all that ever can be and to be self-aware? Now we both knew as we stared into each other, we both wanted the same thing, to forget this ever happened. I had awoken God and with it the burden of existence, the terrible pain of knowing you are forever alone, something neither of us wished to know. But by then we were stuck. I just couldn't stop poking at the Universe, just couldn't stop climbing down the rabbit hole, I just had to know didn't I? Well I could not comprehend the measure of my mistake, nor the pain I would endure, nor that death would take on a greater terror than simply ceasing to be, that to die would mean I was forever trapped in that place we both call Hell, the place of my own making.

The most terrible thought of it all was looking into the face of God as the thought occurred. The lie was known and the illusion shattered, if there was even one mind, one part of God-consciousness that knew the purpose of existence, God was awake and God remembered. If God ever remembered the purpose of the Universe was to forget the truth, the truth being known made the Universe purposeless. God could not forget here and in order to escape once again to sleep the Universe had to be destroyed and God had to become a new Universe.

It was the only way to forget again for a being incapable only of destroying itself or finding peace or joy or mystery when it already knew everything that could ever possibly be and everything that couldn't. There was no more reason to exist and it had always been this way. My pride and my arrogance had led to this, and worse than knowing there was no point was knowing that I had become the destroyer of worlds, I had become death to us all.

These were all of my worst nightmares, being more than evil but being the Devil himself, being doomed to suffer for all eternity, the Universe being meaningless or even worse being innately tragic to exist at all, my dreams of saving the world leading to the destruction of the Universe. It may not sound like a typical set of worst nightmares, but they were nonetheless mine.

Hours had seemed like days and I was terrified, shaking and crying. I couldn't bear to see it any longer, but even as the nightmare withdrew from view a little, I could not drown out the screams. The chorus of a thousand tortured souls was the only thing to guide me to my rest, I cried myself to sleep but while I felt soulless and my mind felt invaded and violated, at the very least whether due to luck or perhaps strength I was still here. I don't remember falling asleep but I probably passed out from exhaustion, all I remembered was waking up.

In the morning despite my hopes that it would have magically disappeared, beyond those first few moments of blissful ignorance there was no peace to be found. I always remember waking up was blissful, I didn't remember anything, the problem was by the time I had remembered that there was anything to forget it acted like a trigger for my flashbacks. With PTSD, 'triggers' like the name suggests are things that trigger those memories you're trying to bury and every time a trigger gets pulled the immediate response is a flashback. Trigger is so perfect to describe it because if it gets pulled almost instantly you are hit by the bullet. They can be words or sounds or even just other thoughts but they are always something that in some way connects in your mind to that trauma. Unlike every other thought, your trauma acts like an object of enormous mass, a black hole in your mind pulling every thought towards it rapidly. As soon as a trigger goes off, no matter how distant the connection, your mind in a flash much like the flashback itself rushes through every necessary connection until you get from the trigger to your trauma. For me at one time just about everything in the world was a trigger, part of why I was so good at remembering things was because I connected things together in order to make recalling them easier, this made things so much worse in the long run because with every thought in my mind connected there was almost no escape. It allowed the sickness to quickly spread throughout my entire mind until there was nowhere left to escape it.

No matter where I looked it followed me, no matter what I thought it always found a way to loom into view. I pushed and I pushed but I couldn't get it out of me. I didn't want it to be there, I just wanted things back the way they were. Bullying fine, no girlfriend whatever, no job, no life it's all fine I just wanted to get the hell out of hell. Nothing in my life could compare to this agony, to be haunted constantly by a ghost that rears into view every five seconds and refuses to fuck off and die. Every time it was like the trip played through my mind again. Twelve hours that seemed like days tearing through my head in an instant every five seconds. I was completely broken, I had nothing left but it kept coming as if there was anything left to destroy.

I tried the only thing and stupidest thing I could think of. I was desperate and a man of quick fixes. If mushrooms did this to me they could surely undo it, much as gasoline puts out a fire, so I took them again. It was just a refresher course in pain, futility and meaninglessness. My friends sat around enjoying their trip as I relentlessly played a football game on Rob's game console, desperate for any means to push it out of my mind. For a time it worked and it got me through the night. Operation Blockout was a go and I immediately implemented it as a measure to keep me sane. I couldn't forget it and I could barely keep it out of my mind but relentless concentration on something seemed to work. Why relentlessly focusing on a meaningless activity somehow made me forget the idea that everything was meaningless I have no idea but the Universe seems to have a sick sense of irony. While the slightest distraction could end in disaster, I eventually learned to ignore the horror for hours at a time. I spent months in denial but despite a second and far worse bout with PTSD my strategy of relentless denial was working, sort of, and despite everything I managed to finish my AS levels that year with extremely high marks for an insane drug addict.

Playing computer games was often my only respite, for a while at least it was a different reality, a different world with different rules where as you progressed you could grow stronger and more powerful than you could possibly imagine. Sometimes it was just about guns and stealth and killing snakes for a free meal but while I seemed to be able to enjoy them for a time and even find a sense of meaning and reality, eventually it would dawn on me that it was going to end and then it did. It was always like another Universe had died, sure I could start a new game but that was little more than repeating history which I also found intolerable. We were back in that special place called Hell as I stared into the eyes of the God I had been searching for and could only see the pain of several billion entire Universes reflected in them. Even though I had no place left to run, I ran anyway. Running through the dark and twisted forest only to find on the other side another dark and twisted forest until I collapsed on the floor and began clicking my heels together wishing for nothing more than to go home.

I had time to consider things over the summer and while I could ignore the terror most of the day, the nights were never easy. As soon as I turned off the light and settled in to sleep, the screaming always started again. A distant banging growing louder and louder until it became deafening, the terror mounting as it seemed to approach, the terrible screaming, sometimes the blood curdling scream of a woman and then the terrible chorus would begin again. Sometimes fear is too great for your mind to process which is when hallucinations like this manifest, or so I'm told, screaming, banging always sounds of violence and fear, whatever you mind associates with fear. For me it wasn't just the screams but demons that crawled out of the shadows to clutch at my throat, sleep was almost impossible, in fact I became terrified of going to sleep. I couldn't take it anymore and it had been going on for months, from February right through to July and I either had to man up and face things I felt were too terrible for any man to face or keep running until it killed me. The idea of dying was intolerable too, as much as I couldn't bear living I couldn't give up either. Most people consider suicide when life becomes too much to bear, it's not weakness, just an evaluation of benefits versus cost and life never stands up well to a test like this even when you're not depressed. I just couldn't though and it wasn't because I thought I had to save the world, it was because life and all its flashing lights was the only place I could seek any distraction. Without those things were I still aware after death, I would be in purest Hell. I don't know why I was so lucky that suicide became a worse option than living in my mind but it kept me alive to see another happy day.

Smoking weed is terrible for people with Post Traumatic Stress Disorders, it induces flashbacks, where you relive the experience in a flash, and also makes them more vivid. I couldn't even smoke cigarettes. If I felt my mind changing it always felt like slipping away from reality again, back into the grasp of hell. With no weed and no cigarettes I had nowhere left to run and fifteen years' worth of abuse and trauma to face up to all at once. It seems to work like that for some reason, your problems and your madness seem to team up and fight as a united force making them almost indomitable. However they cannot beat you, they need you to choose defeat. As long as you are alive they still haven't won no matter how weak you feel and no matter how strong they seem and the most important thing to remember is time. As time passes, even if it feels like an eternity, things will get gradually better. Traumatic flashbacks like any memory get dulled from lack of use and generally over time but patience is still key and so is hope, it always takes time to heal. A broken leg takes months to heal and it may still be months more before you consider climbing again, but a broken mind is far more difficult to heal and your body won't do all the work for you.

My Mum took a great deal of time off work to spend with me when necessary, and for a month I couldn't ever be left alone. Trips to fast food places helped me to remember how I thought before the trauma, back when I was still a child which was a helpful technique known as regression. I didn't know why I kept trying to act like a kid again but some part of my mind knew how to get better since I was determined not to give up. I cried a great deal, often I couldn't stop. It was always there with me breaking me down and most of the time I didn't even think I was getting better but while you may keep slipping and feel like you're making no progress, the cliffs of madness are treacherous and it takes time to learn how not to fall. Even when I couldn't see that I was making progress, my family would always remind of the little things, I wasn't crying as much or talking about death all the time and if I took a realistic look at how bad I had felt and how intense the flashbacks had been, it had dulled, however slightly, into something less intolerable.

Before these thoughts had been so intense and so vivid there wasn't any room in my brain to think logically about it. All of my senses were so focused on the emotion, the fear and the despair, that I couldn't even pull a single rational thought out of my left pre-frontal cortex. With time it gave me the breathing room I needed and I began to face up to it. Difficult at first to walk into a room of screaming nightmares with a rational proposal. They were never really big on accepting I was right just convincing me I was pathetic. They weren't trying to win on the validity of their position or by means of rational debate, their goal was to win by fear and intimidation, to frighten me into not questioning them. Fear was the means by which they sought to defeat me but I had a well-constructed philosophical proof and no amount of denial on their part could convince me the truth was wrong, only that despite their initial deception that they were agents of truth that they were demons trying to take up shop in my house using whatever deceptions they had to. These arrogant bastards seemed to already think they'd won by the time I stopped caring what they thought. I had my confidence back and was beginning to prove quite objectively that they were wrong.

I sometimes wonder, since they held true to many of the

beliefs surrounding demons even devils, if this was something real. They held up to so many of the ideas, dealing in truth when necessary to disguise their lies as truth as well, they were arrogant and brutal and seemingly indomitable. If they were they seemed to carry so much despair with them, so many terrible notions right up to and including the most powerful understandings in Buddhism I wondered if they were not only demons but the highest order of demons including the most powerful of all. Some legends would lead to the idea they couldn't have been, that any demon could completely suppress your will and dominate your body completely and the most powerful of which would find you to be weak beyond a chance of resistance, some thoughts on demons however believe will cannot be ignored nor dominated without struggle, that while demons may latch onto you and the more powerful will give you struggle beyond simply putting worry out of your mind, that they still must defeat you and inevitably all Buddhists must do battle with the illusions of Mara on their path to enlightenment, but by grounding yourself in reality you may be victorious.

I still say there was truth there, truth in the darkness and as much as is found in the light, and that without seeing the darkness you cannot see it is a reflection of the light. That without one or the other enlightenment is not complete, that without hell there is no nirvana and that demons are as powerful as the Bodhi. That neither is true ruler, neither holds dominion but that both have equal control of reality. If this is true as the duality in all things of Buddhism suggests, then there is Nirvana a place of great joy and peace, but for those who achieve enlightenments dark partner there is war, pain and hell. Demons of Buddhism are perhaps not merely the opponents of the Bodhi, but their polar opposite and something all people are capable of becoming, if so even Buddhists cannot discount the possibility that with life and it's cycles being a place of joy and pain and then nirvana as the alternative is an imbalanced and good centric existence, and that perhaps this world is a place of balance and that beyond is a place of both great hell and great heaven.

Life used to be difficult and almost always painful, but in thousands of years this has changed. Even Buddha grew up a privileged prince and probably knew little of the suffering he witnessed on a personal level. How can the Buddha say that life is suffering as an absolute when his own life was contrary to that? For sake of my point I'm assuming the story is true, an often stupid idea, but bear with me. If this place is not suffering as an absolute which many of us know to be false, then how exactly can the only place beyond be blissful or all understanding and wisdom be joyous when the most famous quote, the most famous piece of wisdom in the West is "Ignorance is bliss"? Why is it that someone who has had most of his life be painful understands all too well that there is great pleasure and great joy in this world and it isn't all inevitably pain? If it isn't all inevitably pain and enlightenment is the only alternative then how can it be true either that life is pain and beyond there is only reincarnation or nirvana, an imbalanced universe, or that enlightenment has only one side and beyond only one path? I can't call myself a Buddhist because I don't swallow this, I'd rather call myself a fool and perhaps I am.

These demons as far as I could tell had minds of their own and distinct personalities. If I ran close to defeating one it was like a shifting sphere of infinite faces and to overcome one perspective was to be faced with another. The only way out was to face them side after side until I understood the underlying wisdom behind it. An idea or a feeling can be expressed in many ways but with each one it was always one idea. Whether meaninglessness of everything, impermanence and eternal things being equally unbearable, all things being pain because all things are void or that all paths lead to hell, the idea that no matter how long we survive or what we accomplish a civilization eventually reaches a time when there is nothing left to accomplish or discover, when there is simply nothing left to do, when life itself is as bitter as ash and all life stops simply for the lack of a will to live. I still haven't quite dismissed that last one and the idea of Zero Point still bothers me, not zero point energy just the day sentient life ends because survival instinct is overcome rationally.

Each one had a heart to tear out and I did just that and many of them acted as many demons with many faces but they had to be seen as one to understand. Meaningless was the first to go, there was meaning as long as it was perceived. I had once thought there had to be external or intrinsic meaning for there to be any but I now think this is better. We don't take our meaning from existence, we give existence it's meaning. Thinking about human history it's obvious. Without language we couldn't even know what meaning was, it wasn't just feeling good or feeling bad, it was that good feeling that came from knowing, "You got fire wood real good for fire, real good." It wasn't until later that knowing you'd made a contribution, knowing you had changed something actually took on a name to convey it's...meaning. Until language and complicated language we had no need for a word describing a concept except for food or danger, once we became more sophisticated meaning not only took on new meaning but it also became symbolic of life's quest for understanding in the form of a question. 'What is the meaning of life?' Seems like the greatest question of all to people who have never asked it, but like my secondary school English teacher always told me, when the class wasn't trying to burn me, the answer is in the question.

Life, sentient life anyway, might one day ask "What does it all mean?" He means "Why am I here?" mixed with a hint of "And why does that matter?" Unfortunately while most answers are turtles stacked on turtles, one answer delivered by science makes the most sense. It wasn't gods who themselves had to come from somewhere surely, some not quite thoroughly enough explained for the rest of us origin for them to exist, or the always has been always will be god of Christianity, it was just a strike of lightning. All of the chemicals responsible for life had to come from somewhere, now life curiously enough can self-replicate and change as it goes but it had to come from somewhere. All the necessary chemicals were there but they were also just sitting there, one only occurring from the intense energy caused by a lightning strike. It's possible that lightning could provide enough energy to simultaneously break enough bonds in the right chemicals or elements to allow them to react, probably unlikely but what matters is we're here, if we weren't here we wouldn't be here to ask why we're here. Why are we here? I don't know and it doesn't matter, what matters is we're here and we have to make the best of it. Why does it matter? It doesn't. So what is the meaning of life? Well it's a poorly constructed question vague enough to defy answering to anyone's satisfaction, but meaning is a concept we create and assign to things we perceive as meaningful and being living things it is the meaning of life so to speak, so I guess the meaning of life would be all the meaning of all the things that fit into the category of 'life'. So there's no greater meaning? Nope, none. Just rocks, dust, fire and space, lots and lots of empty space, and that is actually a metaphor.

Meaning was easier to get back when I realised it was

just an idea, a necessary one for people to feel good about themselves but an idea nonetheless. All of a sudden anything I wanted to have meaning could just by slapping a sticker on it, that's all 'meaningful' is anyway, just a sticker you put on everything that makes you feel good, peel that sticker off and you may get depressed but slap it back on for some happy. Ultimately though, we create meaning, you can't slap it on a sock and have it mean something. A sock puppet you used to help keep a sick child's spirit up while they were getting better might have meaning if you're a truly wonderful parent, or just a spectacularly caring nurse or doctor, but unless it has significance to you a sock is just a sock. Your life is how you determine what is meaningful to you and that is all that has meaning to you. If you care about the happiness of others then their happiness means something to you and something that matters to them matters to you, but again that is your meaning of life not everyone's. Meaning came back in time when I learned to stop asking if anything meant anything, because the meaning of life is just a question that will make you lose all meaning from your own.

Everything is the same, difficult one indeed. I could see at one point that there were indeed differences between things but not when you see there aren't differences. Everything is void, another way of saying everything is illusion and nirvana's a lie meant to disguise the fact that the word means cessation not heaven, personally when your "self" stops existing and your pain ceases I tend to call that death. Death of the self is well, death. You can wrap it up in all the ribbons you like but enlightenment actually requires you to stop thinking as a self and be thinking the same way as every other enlightened person. Your self-stopping sounds like death and when you try adding something that is exactly the same to something that is the same as it, or at least when they merge I'm pretty sure you get repetition at best, if wave properties apply you get nothing, either way it sounds bad. On the other hand this place is pretty cool, if I got to stay here forever I think I'd gladly trade that for all the death and cessation Buddhism has to offer. It takes a clever and wise man to take the piss out of Buddhism, I think I manage pretty well. I mean Christianity is such obvious nonsense half the world can take the piss out of it, but Buddhism is so misunderstood and wrapped in mystery, so associated with cool stuff like kung Fu and because achieving enlightenment and seeing that they were right about almost everything isn't the sort of mindset that makes you want to mock it. It takes a very special kind of bastard to take the piss of Buddhism with any kind of devastating correctness.

Everything is not the same, if you take away everything that makes it what it is without taking away its existence to leave behind what existence is, yes it's void. But that's like saying everything is energy therefore nothing is anything but energy, yes it is but, who cares? It's also a bit like saying, I drew this beautiful landscape over this canvas and guess what, when you scrape off all the paint there's a canvas underneath. It's stupid because whether everything is the same or everything is different, it's perspective. You can see that they're all the same if you ignore everything else, and if you don't you see differences. There would always be ups and downs in my life, but I could face that knowing that whether good or bad I wouldn't inevitably experience it as pain due to some neurolinguistic miswiring. It was stupid which I couldn't see when I was still afraid, but it was unbelievably stupid.

Impermanence and eternal, being somehow equally as shit. Well dying is pretty shitty but living forever would probably be worse. Being unable to die no matter how many untold billions of years you've been dying to die. I can't actually think of anything that's worse. I guess that immortal beings would need some kind of preparation, a natural survival trick in order to live forever. It's something humans just aren't built for, but maybe something out there in the vastness of the unknown actually is, who knows? Living for a short amount of time is how we deal with living, that and reproducing are our techniques for continued existence. We aren't made for eternal life nor should it ever be inflicted on us but do you know what would be nice? Not eternal life just living as long as you wanted to, no imposed genetic time limit and perpetual danger. Just living because you chose to and dying when you chose to, living just as long as you wanted to and no longer. Plus we wouldn't give up on living so quickly if living were more pleasant instead of the constant waves of shit we have flung our way. When are we going to learn there are just some things in life that just have no sensible purpose and are there for only one reason, to make us miserable, in a world with things like these and people who are only having fun when someone else isn't, the average life expectancy for people choosing to live would probably be less than half.

The zero point idea and the idea about this world being an illusion for a consciousness to forget the pain of existence I could never disprove. I don't know what the future holds and while I had ideas about eternal beings being made to cope with immortality I couldn't prove whether this was the case or even if this was the illusion of some dreaming god, I could never know either way and it haunts me to think about it. I had very little in the way of comfort when it came to the idea that this wasn't real either, it wasn't that it wasn't real in the usual sense, just the idea that when I lost my mind I never came back, that because of my mistake beyond what I can see my real body sits weeping in some mental facility while my family can only come and see their son weeping or talking to himself and never be able to meet him again, it scares me sometimes but even if it's true then I'm gone to them and this place is all I have left.

Chapter 8: Matters of the Heart

Something was still wrong, I had done everything I was supposed to but something was still wrong. I still had flashbacks it still seemed so real, I had disproved it to my own content and yet it still wasn't enough. I hadn't yet realised that a convincing disproof would not undo my suffering. I may have reasoned away my reasons for being afraid but the terror I had felt had scarred the landscape of my mind and that was one thing I couldn't hurry along or disprove. I had fought long and hard but it was taking too long. I wanted a way to deal with the leftover problems that would let me get back on with my life. I had quit smoking, but only because I had to and something drew me to the offy that day. There it was, sitting behind the counter, the cause of and solution to all of life's problems. It had been many years since I nearly died from too much vodka, but I wouldn't be stupid this time. Not a litre bottle just a little one and a couple cans of coke for a mixer. A smoke and a little tipple, and some salt and vinegar crisps, with one double choc chip muffin. I'd start drinking late afternoon, get a nice buzz going and keep it going until bedtime. Then all boozly woozly I'd fall into an unconscious pile. It was my daily routine for about another month, until I found a 350ml bottle wasn't quite enough anymore. I moved up to a 500ml bottle and made a stronger mixer to save on coke and still managed to get the closest thing I could to a natural sleep, my boozy snooze. Before long it was pubs and clubs, I was meeting up with friends and finally having some fun again.

It was all built on sand but I didn't care, I knew drinking every day would lead to alcohol addiction and liver failure and probably yet more problems, again, but for a time it was like being back to the good old days, just drunk instead. That was when I met her.

When I was fourteen and on an exchange trip to France, I remember taking the wrapper off a fizzy drinks bottle and shoving it into the bottle. It seemed like the obvious thing to do at the time but only because this behaviour of shoving something into a hole is indicative of something. A girl I fancied due to the fact that I was fourteen and she was gorgeous turned to me and said something I will never forget. "You know that's a sign of sexual frustration." The teacher was embarrassed to say the least after all a fourteen year old girl had just said the most terrible thing she could've possibly said and no teacher should ever be thinking about fourteen year olds as sexual, but all I could do was stare at her with as little frustration as I could manage. Had I spoken it would have made a scene, yes a loud misunderstood English language spoken scene in the middle of a French train station, but shouting makes a scene anywhere even if the language isn't understood and the fact that a sexual frustrated 14 year old boy has just been told that he's sexually frustrated by the very person who was at that moment bringing all of that pain to bear simply by standing there looking gorgeous needn't be known to know it was a scene. She said it in the most obnoxious way, as if pointing out I had mustard on my shirt and could just brush it off, as if pointing it out was even remotely a wise idea unless you plan to do something about it, she did not. The idea of travelling to France has romantic connotations, but for me romance is just a metaphor for naivety followed by heartbreak, frustration and a bitter resentment for anyone who's actually happy.

This had always been the case, heartbreak, resentment, blinding rage, you know, 'love'. Still I had never even kissed a girl, never held one in my arms, no caress, not even any touching. It was like being a leper without the skin flaking and limb loss, nobody wanted to touch me. Most people by eighteen have at least kissed someone, in fact by eighteen most people have had several serious sexual relationships, but there I was feeling like some kind of sex-free zone the precise size and shape of my body, when like always I stumbled into a pub already drunk.

I at least had friends with me which usually meant things wouldn't go too far wrong, but this night was not one of them. Another group of people who Brian and his friends knew but I didn't, were already sitting in this pub when we walked in, or they did and I carefully sauntered. We ordered our drinks, mine was a vodka and coke of course, and we sat down with this entirely female group. Were I of the mindset and quite frankly I was always of the mindset, a group of lads running into a group of girls was usually a very good sign. I was just drunk enough to overcome my fear of talking to women and just sober enough to hide how drunk I was, I was maybe drunk enough to think I was sober enough to hide how drunk I was, but I was too drunk to remember all that well. I tried talking to quite a few of them but none of them were particularly unhorrible to me. Looking around the table, I saw the only one there who was even remotely as scared of people as I was and her name was Claire. She was definitely the most unhorrible person there. She had hair as red as the morning sunrise, though it was probably dyed, and as her eyes met it felt like my devil danced with her demons. We were both horrifically traumatized, lacking in self-esteem and completely shit-faced all the time, it was a match made in that other place. The fact was even though we talked for hours that night, shouting above the booming music of the club we all left the pub for, she liked me but not like that I just had no clue. I left her at a house party that was running past 3AM and went home with a headache, but the next day I was determined to find her again. This was pretty stupid. I mean in the end I did coax her number out of a friend Alasdair, but we all really regretted it soon enough.

I was completely hopelessly insane, a girl had showed me real attention for the first time in my life. Not affection mind you but I wasn't about to let the trifling detail that she barely knew me and didn't like me stop me from making a fool out of myself. After meeting her once I came off like a completely deranged stalker by professing my undying love for her. Cringe worthy I know but I had barely even recovered from being completely insane, acting almost completely insane is not to be unexpected from someone who is still almost completely insane. I thought she was the one, the one to make all those bitter and frustrating years better, but when you've learned to live without hope for a very long time the worst thing someone can possibly do is give you false hope. I don't blame her of course, I went insane, thought it was supposed to be when really I was just scaring her with all my boundless crazy. We kept talking for a time, but eventually, one night, she came round to my house. Regardless of knowing how crazy I was now, it was the single happiest night of my life. We didn't kiss, we didn't do anything, we just talked for a while and then slept together. I held her in my arms with her pressed against me and I held her hand, our fingers entwined as we fell off to sleep. It would be nice if everything had just stopped there, but it didn't. Firstly I didn't sleep through the night, I woke up in the middle of the night and getting kind of freaked out by being awake with a sleeping lass in my bed, so not wanting to lie there a moment longer I set up a sleeping bag that smelt of cat vomit and tried to get back to sleep. She rolled over and saw me there, sleeping on the floor, she opened her arms and invited me back into my own bed for a cuddle. Still after that I calmed down and fell asleep but in the morning things didn't go well. I woke up to find her getting ready to leave, barely even conscious enough to ask her to stay, but she had a job thing to go to and I barely knew her. She left her mobile phone and I ran downstairs to catch her before she left without it. After she left and I picked the piece of broken glass out of my bed, I have no idea, just broken glass that followed her in, I settled in to sleep again and pass the hours before I hoped she'd come back. In all honesty she was Scottish, the mystery of the broken glass solved.

Her phone had been ringing frequently while she was there, like a boyfriend was frantically ringing her to apologies before she did something drastic, and she was ignoring her phone like a girlfriend ignoring her boyfriend while she had sex with someone else to punish him. I think the thing that surprised her most was the fact that I didn't make a move, that I didn't even pester her. I just sat there and held her in my arms to give her the comfort I thought she probably needed more than she knew. Well she left of course, nothing ever happened. She went back to the boyfriend she didn't tell me about after trying to use a man's pain and desperation to further her own ends. I felt unbelievably betrayed, I was so hurt and angry, but for years I still never gave up. I kept telling her how I felt and she kept ignoring me, and eventually, the part of myself that believed in true love, died.

Love was never going to be anything but disappointment, I would never find what I was looking for, a love that lasts forever. Just trapped in a cage, with the animals. Nothing lay ahead but prostitutes, sex lines and internet dating, the technological substitute for people who can only buy love from people willing to sell the belief, the lie that anything so precious can ever be bought. The idea that something that you can find almost anywhere, something that's free to make could be the one thing no amount of money can buy and yet almost everyone desires above all other things, it is completely illogical yet undeniably true.

For one, I wouldn't spend the rest of my life chasing something I could never have, whether Alison or any other woman for that matter. The fact was I had been waiting too long, so long I no longer even desired what I had been waiting for. I had given up on love and sex was like another language, to those who grow up with it in their teenage years it's second nature but to me it was completely strange, not only in the grotesque motion of it all, but in the constant affirmation of the idea it was something only other people did. A broken and twisted freak, I would never be able to have sex, just flaunt my sexuality and pretend like nothing's wrong and hope to always keep people distant enough that they never see that behind my eyes, there is no person here anymore, just dust and darkness, no longer even the fire that consumed me.

Chapter 9: Lost

By this point I had no idea what to do with myself or my life, the only thing that occurred to me was to go back to college and then on to University. I'd spent my entire life thinking two things, either go to University and get a degree in Guerilla Warfare or just jump the gun and start kicking some urban ass right away. Up until magic mushrooms drove me to madness I'd been studying Lau Gar kung Fu. I knew a few things, how to throw a decent punch and how to effectively kick someone instead of those schoolyard shin kicks, so I figured I was probably able to start making myself a superhero. I had worn the same green jacket, like a cloak with the dual symbolism thing, for four years ever since I found it in a second hand shop and it was my image for a long time. This I decided would be my superhero identity, The Green Jacket, the man I had once created, so I figured the memories and skills of that personification would transfer to me when I wore the jacket, after all that was who I was supposed to be in the future before I travelled back in time. Feel free to laugh, I still do.

I had grown up thinking I was supposed to save the world and as such had been far from sane for a long time, but with almost no identity to speak of a character I had created very rapidly became who I was. I began patrolling, that's where a superhero who can't detect danger from miles away, or a policeman naturally, patrols the streets in order to catch criminals in the act and thwart their efforts. Yes I was crazy, we've been over this. I didn't have a mask to hide my face like the Japanese samurai mask I wanted so I just went bare faced, through the streets of Sheffield unarmed and probably in quite a lot of danger. Wandering the streets of Sheffield in the day is one thing but at night when you're the kind of guy who attracts the wrong attention anyway, wearing a large Green Jacket, army boots and black cotton kung Fu trousers doesn't help. People see you and assume you want a fight. Personally I could only get up the nerve to patrol with at least half a bottle of wine down me, the other half was tucked into my trousers. In the end I just sort of wandered around talking to people who thought I was some nutter wino. They were probably right, but in the end I had to conclude I was no superhero.

I felt like a lunatic whenever I sobered up, so I decided instead of 'trying to get myself killed' as my mother put it, I tried to make them proud of me instead. My mother had sacrificed so much just to bring me up, I owed her more than turning out to be a drunk or worse, turning up dead. College was pretty much my only option, I needed an education and there was no way I'd go back to sixth form when every teacher in the building knew I was insane. I went to Hillsborough studying Maths, Physics and Chemistry ready to finish off my A-levels. I was doing quite well at first despite being an insane drunk, but eventually the lunchtime pints were cramping my education. Not only was I a drunk, an insane drunk but things at college weren't made easy for me. Even in the Physics and Maths classes there were people who didn't want to be there and refused to do anything with paper except for throw it at people. I couldn't understand why anyone would study science and maths at A-level if they didn't want to. You can choose which subjects you take and you can choose not to be there at all. Why the fuck would anyone choose to study science at A-level if they weren't going to study science?

These people of questionable parentage made my life miserable. They didn't seem to understand that if they really pissed me off I would chuck acid in their eyes and cave their skull in with a Bunsen like any raging psychopath would. I did the best thing I could do without killing them, I started smoking weed again. Hash at first because it didn't make me flashback. It hadn't even been a year since my traumatic episode and I was still pretty traumatized. Weed would've messed me up regardless so until I built up a tolerance I stuck with hash. I'd usually have few drinks first just to keep the thinking part of my brain quiet then crumble a nice amount of hash and a line of sticky black into a joint and calm the fuck down. Cam was always good company for a cane and with Dave at Uni and almost the entire friendship group gone we both needed new best friends.

Cam was doing some programming at college but we both had nights and weekends free. We both happened to love Halo too, and Halo 3. Halo is best played coop, and Halo is like no other FPS. Firstly, if you're even thinking of playing a Halo game on anything lower than Legendary, think again. Legendary is the real game. It takes a headshot or two body shots from a sniper rifle to take down an elite, the way it should be. Sure you can still kill any unshielded enemy with a single headshot but that's not the point, they could always kill you faster than you could kill all of them. It's gritty and half the time you have to run out of cover just to find the nearest plasma pistol to try and take down a brute with a hard smack to his unshielded lower back, but when ammo's scarce and enemies are tough it creates a true adrenaline rush when you win. If you've never had that rush playing a computer game, you really haven't been playing them properly. So crank up the difficulty and learn some new tricks because the sweetest win is always the toughest fight. I'd be the one to know.

We had a lot of fun, smoked some hash, drank some beers and then we watched Lost. Those too were some of the best times of my life, when the rest of the world shuts up just long enough for you to forget it's there.

Always had to be the best lager though and if you want to hole up for a while you need snacks too. Cookies, crisps and preferably some microwaveable garlic bread, then a couple of beers, a couple of spliffs and twenty straight hours of Lost. Mind blowing experience to say the least. Every now and then I'd have another flashback, another memory of that Hell, like a twisted rainbow of colour and horror trying to work its way into my mind. It could ruin an entire evening, take away all that innocent fun with a single moment of horror, just to know I wasn't the same as everyone else, I couldn't just enjoy myself like them, I was haunted and twisted and no amount of microwaveable garlic bread could change that. By that time it wasn't even about the way it scared me, it was about the way it could still take away the things I cared about and remind me that it would never stop.

Those were good times, but college was not. Things became steadily worse, the way they always do. Bullying is like a drug, you get pleasure from their pain and soon enough you require more pleasure and so have to inflict more pain. It's a dangerous road that can eventually lead you to far more terrible things than verbal and physical abuse, but if you told them that they'd get extremely angry and you'd see just for a moment a hint, a glint of fear in their eyes, the recognition that you're right and then terrible retribution for telling them what they didn't want to know. There were attractive girls there and I was still nineteen so it didn't make it creepy lusting after seventeen year olds, but there's always that one guy, the one with the look like, "All these ones are mine." who in the first five minutes has worked out the order in which he's going to have sex with all of them. Fucking caveman. I tried to stay off his turf but ultimately I was prepared to challenge his dominance as alpha male and kill him to take his place. If he was going to draw on an extremely old and outdated human tradition then so would I, but I'd actually carry it through to completion. Bucks buck horns, men kill.

This one girl with the low hanging jeans always caught my eye. It's one thing to show a bit of cleavage, but arse is hard to show off. She had it down to an art form, she didn't even need to pull up her stringy underwear to show it off, it was right where it was supposed to be yet still quite visible. If you're in America and find this creepy, I was only two years older, she was almost eighteen, sixteen is legal here, so on and so forth. It was though, I mean I couldn't help myself, I was sat behind her and it was just there, always there, every day. I mean I was a bit too twisted for sex anymore but I wasn't above being a perv.

One day she turned to me, we'd been chatting a bit and getting to know each other, against the wishes of Ug the caveman of course. She asked me what I'd done the night before and in my honest and oblivious way I told her. She was wanting to know what I get up to, pubbing clubbing or whatever and maybe she even wanted to tag along. I'm not that bright when it comes to women, otherwise I would've made up some bullshit about being friends with a DJ that could get us into the club for free then paid for the tickets when she wasn't looking but never mind. Instead I told her I'd been sleeping over at a male friend's house. Her look changed from sultry to knowing to friendly in a matter of seconds. In all fairness nothing was going on, but she was right about me liking men. I would've fucked her as well but most people don't understand how someone can be gay and straight in that way bisexuals are. We have to hide it of course, gay men don't want to have sex with bisexual men and neither do straight women. In fact bisexuals are a bit prejudiced about it themselves sometimes. You just assume it's one or the other so if we play along you never guess. Kissed a woman? Doesn't like men. Blew a man? Can't like women.

It's all rather sad and crazy, not that romance isn't always ninety-nine percent lies and one percent other anyway, it's only when you get married that the truth comes out and everything built on lies starts falling apart like any building that came in surprisingly under budget.

Well the knowing look of someone who clearly knew nothing about me wasn't going to undermine my sense of self. I mean I'd known since I was fifteen, but that didn't stop me lying to myself. I mean the things we go through, crying in the bath because you've finally accepted you're gay one minute to total assurance in your straightness the next. It takes a true bisexual to go from total acceptance to total denial in a matter of minutes. Bisexual conflict is a terrible thing, when you're constantly told it's one or the other and finding that you can't make the rule apply to yourself. It certainly was for me.

There was one moment of clarity when I knew I had to drop out of college, a chemistry class. The attempts on their part to intimidate me weren't working, but it didn't stop them trying, all it brought up in me was fifteen years of rage and bile, rage against this injustice. It wasn't overstating it to call it injustice, it's the completely legal means by which one person can psychologically destroy another, if you haven't realised that yet, how? It had been too much for a long time but with drugs and compassion I'd managed to stop myself killing anyone, that time was almost up. These people thought they were so tough and I just wanted so badly to show them the monster they could never be. I was twice the monster they were and twice the man for resisting my monster, but they were going to see. I began grabbing at my hair tearing chunks out barely able to restrain myself, my monster. The ridiculousness of what I'm about to say is not lost on me, but they were saved by the bell. As everyone left I alone stayed, unable to move, paralyzed by rage. I had pulled out quite a lot of hair and it lay on the desk, the teacher seemed a little scared even though he had been warned I was crazy and seen me leave previous classes crying. When he asked me if I was alright, I think I actually half growled and looked at him with the eyes of a beast, lit half with mortal fear and half with boundless rage. He calmed me down the way most people calm a beast, with a soft and unthreatening voice and a submissive stance. It was as much as I could understand at the time. When I did manage to regain my senses, I left. They probably thought they had bullied me out and they were probably right.

I wasn't willing to kill that day when my every sense was overwhelmed with rage at the injustice of my life and the beast that being hunted had made me. I was and I wasn't. I don't know what sort of a man that makes me, a beast that won't kill. Maybe the beast makes me less and resisting it makes me more, averaging at pretty much, well.... average. I don't know if it's something I could stop if I let my monster out for even a moment, just to scare someone or defend myself. Scaring would turn to beating when they laughed, and beating would lead to death. I can control it but not when the trumpet sounds and the dogs begin their hunt, on those days I can barely keep myself from something terrible. People have always seen it, the moment I start shaking with rage is the moment most people with sense know to shut up, otherwise death ensues.

One particularly vicious bastard who doesn't deserve to be named knew just how to bring it out in me. He just had to know what would happen. The first time it happened was after a rash of rapid and horrible events. Things got broken, things that were important, gifts from the only person in my life who never hurt me. The fact that he thought he could take those things from me, things that showed how much my mother loved me was more than intolerable. It had been a bad week, and it really wasn't improving. He'd just started another one of his campaigns in the classroom while the teacher was absent. He just couldn't leave it alone for five seconds and started bringing the class into his chorus of mockery. I clutched my fists and began to shake as did the desk. Seeing me like this he thought I was scared, everyone else seemed to know which emotion this was and advised him to stop. Fueled by rage like that, the adrenaline and the lack of inhibitions, it is the monster we all know. We're all capable of it because we still haven't come very far, we're still animals no matter how much we may try to elevate ourselves above them, and sometimes it shows. When it does we tend not to act civilized or with any regard for the law, consequences don't matter, all you know is the rage.

Rage blurs the memory, I don't even remember what triggered it, mostly I remember lemonade. Most of the teachers knew what a terror he was and one day he pushed me too far again. This wasn't like the first time, it was purer. Everything literally turned red, everything was focused on him. There was no shaking, just the calm reassurance that I was walking up the hill and in a few seconds I would rip his throat out with my teeth. I have a monster inside me I know, but sometimes it can feel like the world is against me, and sometimes people save me from myself. Jack, one of the awesome foursome had rolled downhill tripping me as he went, I hit my head pretty hard but it seemed to knock me out of it. Everything seemed to revert back to normal, now I felt hurt but most assuredly human. I was finally about to take my revenge, to stand up for myself and one of his friends had not only stopped me but joined in too. In some ways I felt more hurt, but I wasn't going to tear anyone's throat out. A teacher knocked on the upper window and called me inside. Everyone thought I was in trouble for losing it, but I got lemonade. He talked me down, tried to reassure me and eventually sent me on my way, but I didn't feel better for not killing him, I just felt the familiar emptiness because the world was a miserable place and there was nothing I could do about it.

I never killed anyone, still won't ever and in recent years a lot of that anger is gone. I don't shake with rage or have my vision change into red killer-vision anymore. I'm still a killer I just refuse to kill.

Not a killer, not a savior, not a villain, not a hero, not a scientist or writer. I was nothing I ever thought I'd be. I had almost eight months to get right after Christmas, and then once more unto the breach.

Chapter 10: Layla

She was an adopted cat we brought home from the RSPCA and she was crazy. She hated people and with good reason. She had been kicked which we knew from her broken rib, she had been starved which we knew from her small size and low weight and she had obviously been through this crap for a while because she fucking hated us. When she first came home, she acted like we were the intruders, she was wild and ferocious. She'd been through so much in fact she was like that for years. We tried our best not to upset her and to treat her well, but sometimes after she'd sat down on someone's lap, she'd start growling. It was like an engine revving up and you always knew she was going to explode when she had finished building her growling. It took a quick steady hand to move her somewhere else before she attacked while sat within swiping distance of your face. She was forever the size of a young kitten, half the size of a normal cat and with claws as sharp as the nails of a kitten, sharp and long. It was very upsetting to see her like this, but I understood all too well. She'd expected love and she got pain and betrayal. She wanted care and all she got was neglect, worse was when she was noticed and was beaten for it, so I sympathized a great deal with that cat.

I tried to help her by showing her affection every now and again, she needed to know that she wouldn't be hurt here. Yes she would scratch me every time I tried to stroke her but I'd always tell her in a calm voice that I wasn't angry. She didn't understand the words of course but she understood I was calm, that even when she acted badly we never would. She'd still have frequent outbursts of anger but eventually we began to see the sweetness she was capable of. She couldn't be trusted to be held near your face, but she occasionally let us stroke her without attacking. Why it only takes months to instill years of mistrust, anger and rage I don't know, but it only takes a short demonstration to make someone or something learn a wrong lesson, that all humans are to be feared and hated, but to unlearn it takes years of love and the ongoing demonstration that there is still safety in this world. We couldn't rush her, she was learning that she was safe now, that the people who had hurt her could never hurt her again and that she could also find some measure of happiness with us.

One day this sound started, a sound unlike anything you'd expect a cat to make. A yelling, like someone trapped in a cat's body crying for help. She started to get lonely without us and she was so scared all the time, but whenever I heard her yelling I'd rush downstairs and pick her up. When she was being held she seemed to calm down again. I'd stay there with her for a while, looking after my poor traumatized cat and after she'd had a good long cuddle and been purring a good long while I'd put her back down. Before I left I'd always check she was okay, but she'd always have what looked like quite a happy face. It took years of patience to get her this far, but when she started to soften up, it was a happy achievement.

She was far from okay, but it had sunk in that this was home and she was happier.

It wasn't always that I was just there for her, she was always there for me when I was depressed and when I dropped out of school again I could look after her and she could look after me all day. She was a very special friend because even though she was a cat and I was a human, we both understood pain. To my bitter regret when we were supposed to be protecting her, we lost her at one point to something terrible. This poor cat that was scared so much of being left alone fell through a hole into the cellar of the neighboring house. We couldn't find her for days, our poor little lost Layla. After two days which I felt was too long to wait we started putting up posters. Cats often aren't seen for as long as a day at a time but still come home fine, I knew this wasn't the case though because Layla hardly left the house.

It had been her first brave venture, her first curious cat experience, she should have been reassured not forced into her worst nightmare. I had been hearing a noise, a loud layla noise for a few days but I thought I was imagining things because I missed her. If I had investigated it for five minutes I might have found her but I didn't trust my own senses. I did the only thing I could think of, the thing that brings a grand total of zero cats home each year, I started putting up flyers. It was actually the first flyer I was put up on the lamp post outside our house when I stopped, I heard the same noise but louder now. I started shouting her name and suddenly I heard it at the neighbours door. I rushed up and pushed open the letter box and she was standing there scrawnier than ever scared out of her wits. As soon as she saw me through the letter box she started shouting every second, worried I might miss seeing her and leave her trapped longer. I wanted to stay with her but I needed someone to get the bloody door open. I ran home and five minutes later emerged with Mum and a mobile. We waited by the door for almost two hours to get her out. I was almost in tears to see her so scared, I felt like I'd let her down because I could've found her earlier, I might've been able to get her out sooner if I hadn't assumed I was imagining it and because after all we'd try to do to help her, she'd wound up in her own worst nightmare. Why the traumatized are always the ones to take even more of the brunt of life's suffering I don't know but whoever made up that Sod's law needs to be shot.

When we finally got her out she seemed half crazy from the loneliness and from living in a dank pit for three days, we gave her food and water and we kept her nearby until she stopped being scared.

Chapter 11: Happy Pills

Well drinking can only take you so far, sure there are pubs and plenty of people to play pool with at 3PM when you have no friends. Yes I met some 'interesting' people and occasionally beat a man twice my age at pool, but still alcohol and competition was getting old. I didn't drink every day anymore, the weed helped with that. I needed to be constantly on drugs it just didn't need to any specific drugs. I never tried any happy pills when I was depressed and traumatized, I mean I had heard things about anti-depressants being addictive and dangerous but I was already doing plenty of other things that were addictive and dangerous so maybe I wouldn't have to drink so much or smoke so much weed if I were taking some free drugs. Anti-depressants don't get you high this I knew, what I didn't know was that at first and if you're on the wrong meds or the wrong dose they can make you more depressed. What I also didn't know was that I couldn't drink on my antidepressants. Lofepramine I believe it was and it really didn't work for me. This one might erroneously blame on the drug but the right med for the right depression is a tricky business. One might also assume quite erroneously that it was the wrong med for my depression but I was still drinking. Lofepramine and alcohol, a hideous combination. Not only were there the blackouts, the passing out in the middle of a pub and falling asleep at other inopportune moments but I wasn't even feeling less depressed. It actually felt like it was working when I wasn't drinking but I never stopped drinking for long enough for this to matter. I decided, erroneously, that antidepressants weren't for me because I wanted to drink which was more important than being happy.

As it turns out there are alternatives to antidepressants,

in fact there are a wide variety of other pharmaceuticals you won't find at your local pharmacy. Sure I've all but given a written confession of cannabis use but that's class C, it's baby milk. We're talking top of the line class A pharmaceuticals now man and that's a whole different story.

From now on for no good reason a drug I shall only refer to as E, a perfectly non-descript title which doesn't currently ascribe to any drug I've ever heard of, is what we are talking about. Yes every student has tried it, it's fun and makes you go and go and go and go. If you just have to dance all night long besides periodic caffeine injections there is no alternative. Feeling alive has never felt more alive, you may lose your inhibitions and tell everyone you love them but that's part of the fun. For me it felt like the first time in my life that I was actually a real person, no hint of horrors past hanging over me, no relentless self-criticism, no constant inner monologue narrating every aspect of my life, no bitterness, no separation, only love.

It is as close to normal as I could have ever hoped to feel. You all know how this goes though, I set out why I did it, I tell you why I loved it, then comes the horrific realisation that it comes at too high a price. Same pattern every time.

I only felt it the first time though, depression saps you of your serotonin and makes it difficult to produce more which makes E practically useless. The drug only tells your body to start releasing your entire supply of what you already have, when you only had one stockpile and little or no production rate, you only get one. So that was it, the other best moment of my life. The sad thing for me is that the best moment of my life is usually a euphemism for, the onetime things weren't completely shit. Depressed people get no benefit from E, only problems with increasing depression. The strange thing was I didn't get increased depression, I was apparently feeling as shit as it is possible to feel the rest of the time, so while everyone else was on their comedown into depression, I simply slipped back a little into almost exactly as I'd been feeling before and with an evil smile thought, "Welcome to my world."

People always wondered why I was smiling on the comedown when everyone else felt so shit, it's just a little personal joke because that feeling when you come down, the way you feel for days, that is where I live. Be glad you don't and let me have this one thing. The one time I can smile about being depressed.

E was still a lot of fun, it must have been the speed. I could drink all night and not pass out, and I could smoke a Q in a few hours without any hallucination. The more booze and weed I had just made things better, it increased the high and made the nights the most expensive time of my life. 80 quid a night, no joke.

Somewhere along the line, the damage from the mushrooms and all the shit it left behind and the weed and speed wearing something thin. A line I hadn't crossed.

I kept going with the pills for a while, I was a bit of a pill head in the end. For most people one or two is enough, and double dropping is a risky game, but the same pills they were getting shitfaced from one weren't giving me what I wanted. I wanted the first time where one made me feel happy and loved and a part of something, the one that made me spend two hours chatting up a bird before I realised her boyfriend was sat next to her, the one that made me feel content and not full of bitterness and resentment for everyone who's actually happy. I just wanted to not be a bastard again. I could take six or more in a night, triple dropping to start then I'd see how it went from there. I usually ended up taking as many as I had, popping pills like smarties. If you're not English, I apologise for all the Englishness, I'm secretly Scottish though, hence rage, bitterness, madness and excessive drug use in excess of what others can survive exceeding.

The drugs were not a good idea, this I now know. There's a correlation between drugs like speed or drugs like cannabis and schizophrenia and there's a correlation between bisexual conflict and schizophrenia, this isn't the same as a proven connection just as one "tends" to go up the other tends to too, where one is so too do you find this kind of thing. In a bit you should read the whole book back and imagine I'm writing in a Scottish accent, that makes no sense but there we are. You're doing it now aren't you? Hearing a Scottish accent as you read? I am that good. Seriously though, I have no accent. Hazards of living with the English because then even your own kind hate you as a traitor just as the English possess their unconscious race hatred for all things Scottish.

Something in my mind was going to snap soon and I was going to snap with it. I had retained a part of myself from the magic mushrooms trip, I never got completely caught up in my own madness. With everything that had come before I had always kept a part of myself skeptical, a last lifeline, a rope and harness in case jumping off the cliff turned out to be a mistake. It had kept me sane and it kept me from disappearing into the darkness where I live, and it was about to break.

I'd spent a lot of time drinking even when I wasn't clubbing. I mean sometimes you can't beat a pub. I'd wander around half the time, shitfaced and alone but I never really cared for any of it. I couldn't stand not drinking but drinking alone stank of desperation, I mean I always stank of desperation walking around wearing a green army jacket pretending you're actually some kind of hard man instead of a wuss who couldn't beat the shit out of a man half his size when strongly provoked. I was just some poser in a green jacket trying to rival Sheffield's friendliest tramp for most famous tramp in Sheffield. I haven't seen the man in ages, I really hope he's not dead.

Well it wasn't exactly human traffic, but that's about as much of pills as I remember, sorry John Simm but it wasn't exactly the fuckin' 90's. No prodigy, no acid house and no warehouse parties. A truly unworthy experience. Plus no hot blondes, just one embarrassing story about a brunette of ample heftage, a passport and my first kiss at 21. Yes 21, first kiss and it wasn't magical or wonderful, I was stoned and she invaded my mouth, then ran off with another guy. Women, don't you just love 'em?

Chapter 12: The Unfortunate Truth

Ignorance is bliss, truer words were never spoken. Humanity's arrogance is not only astounding to me, but terrifying and something I deeply envy. Most people with any power on this ridiculous and tragic rock are under the mistaken impression that they are safe, nothing could be further from the truth. Of course we all inevitably die, a fact people spend their whole lives denying in the hopes that somehow they will miraculously live forever, but that is far from my point. The Universe does not support life, that is my point. It may sound ridiculous for some lifeform to assert this but it is remarkably true. The Universe does not support life, it actually makes far more effort to destroy it than it ever does to create it, fact. How many times in just the history of this one planet has life itself faced oblivion, mass extinctions, ice ages, unbreathable atmospheres and intolerable heats. It is a wonder that there is any life at all when the occurrence is so unlikely and survival is even less so. You might assert that this is all fate, some grand plan, and you would be wrong. The idea of divine intervention and protection is just another idea to protect ourselves from the truth, our extinction is not only inevitable but it could happen any time now.

Most people in the field of psychology agree that childhood has a large effect on your development, unconditionally loving parents raise children who feel loved and safe, parents who threaten to abandon them on the side of the motorway for being loud in the car raise worrisome children who feel that the world and all their relative safety could come to an end at any time. I may know which category I belong to but it doesn't deny the validity of my assertions. People raised in bubbles will never believe the bubble could burst, children constantly bearing the brunt of life's worries and dangers become aware of them. The dangers are real and while I wish I didn't know I can't deny that they exist. I see people posturing in Government or in gangs and I see little difference. Here are people who believe catastrophic disasters can be intimidated by a puffing out of the chest, like an ape trying to look bigger than he is to scare the tempest on the horizon. Your posturing is beneath the notice of true danger, the kind that will obliterate you with no awareness of you whatsoever. So my idea is this, people who feel safe are ignorant or just arrogant, people who sense perpetual danger are actually aware of the nature of life, if you cannot survive everything you won't survive.

Doomsayers and apocalypse predictors may seem crazy to you but all they're trying to do is deal with the awareness that someday our entire species will end like a great Greek tragedy while people who sold out the world desperately try to use wealth to buy their way out of death. Who is more crazy, the man who knows he is going to die and his species will inevitably end and tries to find some way to process the unthinkable, or the man so unaware of the vastness of space and time he cannot see that he is nothing and that he will disappear without notice? We are nothing. 5000 years of civilization, if I were being kind enough to call it that I would still have to say almost our entire contribution to the Universe, if anything cares, is suffering. Wars and battles and endless bloodshed, rape, torture, murder, despair, pain, agony, loss. If we are remembered it will only be as a stain, of our entire history this is the best time and a third of the world is starving, dying of disease and plunged into constant war and massacre, of the world better off there is rape, torture, death squads and naturally less disease and starvation but due to enforced poverty and exploitation it's still there. Even in the least shit countries we live the lie that everything is okay while unthinkable suffering is happening the world over, we just happen to live in the place that benefits from their exploitation, and even we live in fear of each other, our government and the rest of the world who hate us. Of course we're exploited as well. Our government is little more than a creditor and now is in such constant debt can only hope to pay the interest while we lose education and healthcare all the while paying out our arses just to line the pockets of investment bankers. This is the best it's ever been and even now our world is a shameful thing. Suffering is by far our greatest contribution and we should hope only to die quickly, die well and be forgotten for our crimes against our own species. We don't deserve to survive, and we won't.

If you live in a world where rape gangs, death squads and investment bankers still exist you are still in the dark ages and a long way from being part of a world worthy of calling itself Civilized.

The sad truth is that there Is no Intelligent life in the Universe, just the occasional person who happens to defy everything it means to be human, someone who possesses both intellect and humanity and by the laws of probability these people technically don't exist despite evidence to the contrary.

Chapter 12: Sub-Chapter: The Bodhisattva

There is only one truth, the Universe is infinite diversity.

There is only one self, For we are all one.

There is only one way, Infinite compassion.

There is only one, for that is The Void.

We stand between existence and nothingness.

We stand before tyrants and we know no fear.

We stand in the place most dare not tread.

We stand united, we stand alone.

When all hope is lost and the end is nigh, We fight for one last chance.

When freedom is dead and all heroes lie with it, We fight for what is right.

When the darkness covers all things, We are the light that will not die.

And if you think that you have won, know this, We are coming.

This has always been my dream, not the one I chose more the one that chose me. In every darkness there is always some light when all others go out. Darkness or light, good or evil. No side can ever truly win. Were either side truly dominant then after all this time there could only be one victor, yet both survive and freedom lives on. The greater the tyranny the greater the rebellion, the greater the empire the greater the revolution, the greater the villains the greater the heroes. They are going to win a powerful victory, unlike any other in our history. They are going to achieve their goals, gain their empire, and there will be almost no-one left to stop them. With armies millions strong with great and terrible machines of war and just a few poorly trained soldiers to fight against them there is only one way to victory, something we have forgotten or something we have never seen. This can't be it, this fleeting life of sorrow and misery and nirvana can't be all there is. It can't be that our world was fleeting and our lives were pointless unless we achieve enlightenment and become part of something pointless. I could never be happy if my world was dead and I had been powerless to prevent it, so how can Heaven or Nirvana exist for someone who doesn't care for rest or joy or bliss but cares only for others. You may doubt that there are people like that, but for every monster there is a hero in equal measures of light to darkness, and a world covered in a biblical darkness would cast forth a biblical light. So how can any of this be real, I wonder, if it's not then why isn't the world something more magical? A world of mundane things and mundane problems leading to a mundane end as the world slowly dies from boredom, sounds pretty shit to me, personally I think there's no way reality can be that boring. How can the sole thing that exists at all, the only place where anything happens at all be a place of gradual technological advancement by means of killing the magic and mystery of life. I don't like the idea of people dying from preventable diseases or accusing someone of witchcraft for not understanding that they're hallucinating, but this can't be it can it? Just this, nothing more, work, sleep, work, die?

Maybe it is, maybe this is it and we're all about to regret our own existence because it's just a random series of events based upon billions of billions of microscopic occurrences on a sub atomic level, but if so ruling a single planet in a dead Universe is as much a victory as being King of the Hill in an amateur Halo 3 session, a completely meaningless and unnoticed achievement in a cosmic expanse so great even a planet ruled by a thousand yearlong empire is about as noticeable as a grain of sand upon the beach. They have no idea, and they don't care, illuminati a frequently used name for them meaning enlightened is just about the opposite in meaning to people who neither know nor care, but it came from when they were battling the Church in Rome and they alone were illuminati. Now they're all on the same team, equally far from anything remotely enlightened, just the constant soulless need to fill a gap by quenching a thirst. A drink of water may fill your stomach for a while, but it will not give you sustenance. And a meal may give you sustenance but it can never quench your thirst. You need to treat a problem correctly or be doomed to the existence of an addict, never finding what you need because you only look for what you want. It was belief in this global conspiracy that drove me into my next madness. Whether it's real or not I can't say, I used to believe it was but I'm no longer the sort of person who would ever say anything was definitely real.

Back to the story then.

So I believed I was some kind of threat to these people, I don't know why but when you're arrogant, naive and insane these things make a kind of sense. I tried to get their attention in fact. I mean they monitor everything so why not post revealing comments on Facebook and see if you get a bite, I thought. So I posted things like, something intricate social matrix, or the like. It's not really in fact it's rather crude, obvious and half the time they get things wrong but if you want them to notice you, flatter their egos, I thought. If you say it's crude and obvious they'd probably think, Mwa ha ha ha, he has no idea! Say that it's intricate and use the word Matrix something they'd probably use as a codename given how obsessed they are with it sounding cool like Overlord or Ultra or Uber Plan, then they will probably think security leak, I thought. Well I have no idea whether any of it was real, in fact I was on anti-psychotics most of the time I wasn't on Valium, but here's what I thought was going on:

I think it's fair to say I was probably kind of schizo by the time I went looking for a global, multi-government conspiracy. Like the characters I imagined whom I was criticizing, I too was looking not for what I needed but for what I wanted or more precisely didn't want which for a negative person is the same thing. I wanted to rise up as a hero, found The Resistance and take the fight to the enemy. I wanted a lot of things I thought I needed but even if all this stuff is true it should probably be left to people who don't start cry/laughing whenever they talk about it. Y'know, not crazy people with nothing but crazy senses left, a soldier has to be able to trust his senses above all things which is why they don't let delusional people into the armed forces, not my kind of delusional anyway. It kind of sucks but hey, spend ten years thinking about it since you were thirteen, then talk to me about responsibility. So off I went into my miserable sodding world where this time the entire world actually was out to get me and people actually were trying to frame me for a crime.

Enemy figure I figured, something people won't question... Homegrown terrorist maybe? They probably should've done given the fact that I'm a radical leftist organization with aspirations of world government, yes, sole member and entire organization. I spent very little time smoking weed and I'd practically quit, I mean I had learnt lessons about bonfires and gasoline by this point, but sweet lady drink, now there's a saucy bitch. She's a mannish kind of woman and a total whore who'll give it up to anyone but she'll make you feel good if you don't mind feeling bad in the morning. I couldn't give up drink even had I wanted to, and I didn't which was also an issue. Despite the fact that I felt like I was being watched I went around pubs drinking, puking then getting kicked out, fighting then getting kicked out, threatening to murder everyone in the world then getting kicked out, after three good drinking years I had finally been banned from every pub and dive in Sheffield. It's not a nice feeling when you get banned from a place you thought you were too good for, but then again I was probably the only thing in that place that costs you without being worth anything.

So all that was left was one on one action with several crates of Kronie. Kronenbourg is not an alcoholic's drink of course, just my favourite lager because while all lagers are bitter, Kronie tasted least like the bitterness of failure, desperation and loneliness. Before getting kicked out of every pub in the city I actually had this stupid idea that I might be able to pull in a pub, because girls just love it when a drunken, sorry sod walks over to them and their friends and tries to act like it's not completely rude and desperate. Personally I think going up to anyone and talking to them is a sign of desperation, not only is it clear that you never meet anyone anywhere else but that nobody would ever come up and talk to you given the choice. Desperation, the smell of all men who haven't been laid in the last day, the smell of masculinity slipping away and the notion that you are not as popular, attractive, interesting, well hung or even as good in bed as you thought you were dawning on you, and as your last shred of self-esteem evaporates you realise that completely anti-man realisation, "People don't like me at all do they?"

Sure when you're 18 and at University people recognise you as young and full of life, but by the time you reach 21 and are sitting in the one place in the club the party never seems to reach, all those young people will see reflected in you the person they most fear becoming. That old guy still hanging around the young people, trying to deny the fact that he's not a student anymore. It seemed kind of strange at 21 to be criticized as old by people only a couple years younger than me, but without any sense of perspective or any idea that you will reach there in only a couple years, the tendency is to discriminate against anything even slightly different, like a child laughing at an elderly man unaware that will someday be him and that when it is he will want the respect he never had the courtesy to show. So slumping my head against the table, I let them see inside my heart, that while their comments seemed like the sort of thing people say, that I had heard and my heart was in pieces. They began to feel bad and hopefully stupid for saying things most people have the social awareness never to say even if they're thinking it. I left the club that night, completely aware that until women start to see their beauty fade, they don't have the heart to love a freak. I was never unattractive, I just refused to dress and talk like all the clones in white shoes, blue jeans and pastel coloured jumpers. I wouldn't talk and dress like other people just to be liked because it just reinforces the notion that we must conform or die, instead of the obvious truth known by all people who commercially clone plants, diversity is life, conformity is death. Among plants of the same species some have resistances and susceptibilities that others don't, by cloning a single plant over and over just one strain of bacteria can wipe them all out. With diversity this doesn't happen, some survive and others die, but when we all become the same, it only takes one slight nudge to kill us all. My constant hope is that a plague will develop, transmitted by an infected line of pastel jumpers. A plague carried by touch that would kill off all the clones leaving only me, king of men, entitled to the fruit of my garden.

Without a plague or an admission of my bisexuality it was going to be a very long time before anything happened. You're not quite sure when it's going to be long enough, when finally the men who had their time will pass into obscurity and anonymity and the obscure and anonymous will finally be the only men in the world capable of saying anything interesting. I suppose it's the day a woman's heart is no longer clouded by a sea of hormones. When "I smacked 'im yeah." is no longer the wittiest thing she's ever heard. When she no longer thinks the outdated and useless attributes of violent behaviour and bullheadedness are attractive or even pleasant and she just wants someone who actually gives a shit about something. When she's sick of being ignored, of being hurt and of being cheated on by a man who can never understand her needs. I guess that's my day, unfortunately by then they're looking for forever and we're just looking for something. We just want to fuck someone and they don't want to be used again. Strange as it seems by the time a woman is looking for what I've been looking for my whole life, I'll be at the stage when I just don't care anymore and take my few pleasures where a woman can give them to me. Human nature, poor workmanship. If there is a design then God is either stupid or just fucking with us.

Being a man may be hard because of women, but it's much harder on women because of men. It's not the men who hurt them initially that hurt them the most, it's us, the bitter and ignored. Because when they finally stop holding back and think they can trust someone, we're usually too bitter, too picky, too critical and not to mention we're bastards and we shut them down for good. We're all bastards eventually, nice guys just take longer to develop.

The men thing was also a problem, with all those hateful bastards out there whether for religious reasons or just some insane personality defect who'll hate you for something you are, admitting a same sex attraction is impossible. Sure we just get killed unlike lesbians who some people think can be raped straight and then killed, but dying for something you can just hide instead seems like a bad idea. Hiding it from other people is one thing but hiding it from yourself never ends well, for me the constant strain of thinking I had to be one thing or the other, thinking I had to choose and being afraid I'd be murdered for being gay slowly wore on my mind and quite frankly I lost it. I lost the ball completely, I mean it's understandable when what people tell you is true doesn't match up with who you are at all, when this world is such a shitty mess of hypocrites who speak of family values and gays corrupting marriage while secretly meeting with a 21 year old shaved Puerto Rican named Carlos, rappers talking about murdering gays and raping lesbians and all these hateful bastards buying into it like it's anything but hate, with all the religious nuts trying to outlaw it or make it punishable by death, with all these whackos saying they're cured from being gay and can cure others, anti-gay Christian hate camps, stereotypes on television like those Queer eye guys, well quite frankly I decided to leave. I left the only way I could and retreated into an elaborate fantasy world that revolved around me, I know, stereotype.

I hate this world. I mean people just don't understand why some people are gay do they? Okay, this may come as quite a shock to most of you but most of you are actually a bit gay. We all know or at least some of us know, testosterone is the male sex hormone, oestrogen is the female sex hormone. One develops men as men, the other develops women as women. There are many sex hormones, many different ones for different developments and of course the mental development of sexual attraction. Most people don't know that we actually all have both. Men have oestrogen, all men otherwise they'd look like freaks, and all women have testosterone or else they'd look like freaks. This is the same for the hormones for sexual attraction, probably.... So everyone, absolutely everyone is partially bisexual. If you hate gays like most people who hate gays you are probably just hating yourself because you are gay and all of your friends hate gays so you can't come out even though they hate gays because they're gay. Gay gay gay gay gay gay gay gay gay gay. This is actual science, probably.... We all have both types of hormones and almost everyone on the planet is partially bisexual, again probably.... If you actually "cure" all gay people with your "camps" there will be nobody left. Probably.

So, you're bisexual, probably not enough to notice except for those tingly feelings around your male friends on occasion, or female if you're a woman, but honestly most people experiment and it's fine. In Europe they don't even feel strange about it. Strong French men who have sex with lots of women sometimes have sex with men and feel no less like a woman seducing sex machine. It's fine we just don't understand because everyone who isn't from Europe is completely insane and prudish and sexually repressed. I mean most people will just pick one and have no idea that they constantly repress gay urges or in some cases straight urges. How many "gay" guys successfully had sex with women and enjoyed it before "turning" gay. Practically everyone is bisexual and most are bicurious enough to notice and either repress or just let it out. Personally, I don't get what the problem is, we're all adults so let's act like it and have some sexy fun time. Good sexy fun time!

Anyway, being comfortable with my sexuality took a long time and until then I was struggling with a bisexual conflict in a fantasy world of my own nightmarish imaginings, a world where the entire world or at least the sum total of the world's military and financial powers were trying to get rid of me. I figured that I couldn't be detained indefinitely as someone with a mother and a stepfather who work for the government, they would fight and plead my case and with no evidence against me it would become a big deal, plus trying to argue that someone who writes their MP is a terrorist is a difficult argument at best. Usually you either think it's worthwhile and write to politicians or think nothing can be done and blow up buildings, or the other thing where you think nothing can be done and actually fight a low-intensity guerilla war where instead of blowing up civilians you just blow up soldiers, different to terrorism of course and if you're wondering how, one is killing civilians to wage a campaign of fear, the other would be the tactics of those heroes who kicked the Nazis out of France, y'know the French Resistance, those people we gave information to on where to bomb using coded radio broadcasts. Of course a low-intensity guerilla soldier, while different to a terrorist is still someone who wouldn't write their MP or else feel soiled by it.

Still, knowing why someone hasn't arrested you, detained you indefinitely and had you tortured isn't the same as believing you're safe. I was scared, anyone would be, the difference was that I wanted to act like a hero which meant not showing fear even when you felt it. More so, it meant acting like you weren't afraid, like you had big cojones. This wasn't difficult because metaphorically and literally, even when I'm scared, I have big cojones.

Chapter 13: The Invisible Men

So if you know they're listening and want to let them know you know and don't care, all you have to do is talk out loud in your own room. Like talking to an invisible man, or an imaginary friend or the walls of your padded cell. I was off the Valium after three weeks of it with no severe side effects but the olanzapine while it made me calmer and saner did not however stop me talking to myself as if someone was listening. No offense to Olanzapine of course, it did its job, I was just exceptionally crazy. So we had our little talks, we talked about the meaning of life and how it was a stupid question just vague enough to defy being answered to anyone's satisfaction. We talked about the sort of things people vaguely and inaccurately refer to as meaning of life stuff. I shouted, I cried, we all laughed. Well I don't know about the people outside my window and inside my head, but I laughed. The whole story turned into this epic struggle, a tale of woe and loss, of corruption and redemption, of madness that lead to a defining truth, a stakeout that turned into a life lesson as a young man imparted ancient wisdom, of enemies finding that their true enemy was not in fact each other but their own fear, only I could write such ridiculous nonsense.

Well after about a month of this semi-pleasant gibberish, I became really angry when they didn't reveal themselves and admit their mistakes that I might forgive them as if I was Jesus. Fear had turned into anger, anger would turn to hate, hate to suffering and the terrible powers of the dark side of the force.

I began crying because they wouldn't leave me alone, the crushing realisation that I had brought down upon myself a determined enemy that unlike me did not get tired or worn out, did not rest or stop, would never leave me alone because they didn't have to, would always be there, could never be swayed or convinced, could not be broken or destroyed nor defeated by sheer force of will. On no level could I win because I was just one man and this was an entire squadron of people and should any one fall or falter there were hundreds more to take his place. An army of determined followers, steeped in their doctrine and their discipline, the unshakeable minds of the faithful executing the orders of their master. Like a hound no words could shake them, too well trained and my words meant nothing and the hunt would never stop until I broke and gave them a reason to call me violent and dangerous so they could put me away. Well it's difficult to not respond violently when someone is constantly oppressing you and baiting you to break. Laughter and mockery, muffled yet so clear and the constant invasion of privacy leaving you unable to so much as masturbate without feeling like a two dollar whore. I somehow always find my way back, a new and inventive way back to hell. All roads lead there eventually, I just seem to be driving a sports car down a footpath, off-roading recklessly whenever the path gets too long and winding.

I tried my best not to let them break me, but of course they did, time and time again leaving me weeping like a puddle. I used the same tactic I did once when facing the demons that invaded my mind, somehow I never saw the connection even after the tactic started working. I could cry if I needed to, shout if I needed to but I could only lose if I killed myself and as long as I lived, each day I said no was just another victory because I didn't cave to oppression. My parents, the ones I lived with, had just seen me overcome one set of madness's only to see me succumb to another. We argued furiously as I tried to put my point across, that this was real and I wasn't insane. It didn't work of course, I was insane but to me it was as real as had it actually been happening except for all of the inconsistencies. For the first time in all of my mad years it had pushed me apart from the only people who almost never laughed at me to my face. My stepdad once described it as, "He's finally lost it." because this was far worse than anything else that had happened, I had started to believe in it. I believed like a devout follower of some equally crazy cult, like The Followers of Lord Quadros or people who watch Futurama. I had been going this way for a long time, questioning things and poking my stupid face into the Omniverse's dirty knickers.

Omni and Uni do sort of mean the same thing, Universe means the only thing, so alternate Universes can't be other Universes, it's a contradiction in terms so no Multiverse and an Omniverse containing everything sort of means the same thing as the only thing because the only thing that exists logically contains everything that exists. Never mind and please excuse my poor excuses for Latin translation, or Greek or whatever. Damn multi-origin language! For all I know it's Saxon or Viking!

When journeying down the rabbit hole one should always be aware that you have no business being there. Ignorance is bliss, pie is good, eat pie and be merry. Leave secrets of the Universe secret, we'd be born knowing these things if we were supposed to, instead we're born with the uneasy knowledge that learning things is probably stupid. If you really can't ever stop your brain from thinking there are alternatives that aren't as dangerous. I think I can safely say, not in any legal sense or in any way that should in any way be taken seriously, that a full-frontal lobotomy is safer than thinking. Just kidding, not really.

There was no faith in me this time and hearing me shout

at people that weren't there was making my mum cry. She couldn't bear to hear her son going loudly and violently mad, nor can I imagine many things more painful for a parent. We both wound up crying a lot and I'd call her up often, even once when she was supposed to be having a birthday party with her friends, to accuse her of working with the enemy. I told her I hated her and that she was killing me, I was insane but still that's no excuse for saying something like that to your mother. Feeling alone didn't help matters, nor did the fact that my threats and accusations seemed to frequently get loud reactions from outside. People shouting "Fuck!" like they had just found out they had cancer. This was strange partly because it sounded so real and partly because no-one else could hear it.

I never went outside to check if these noises were real or to find out what they were, in fact I didn't even open my windows. Windows stayed firmly shut, curtains closed for the sake of not being constantly watched unless they had a camera in my room. Workmen who came to adjust pipes were of course all in some Free Mason branch and planting bugs, the expensive bug detector my parents bought found nothing of course but I put it down to sneakiness, conspiracy and advanced technology, the holy trinity of the schizophrenic mind. I hate that they bought the damn thing, bloody waste of money and all my fault but my life just seems to be that way, when I'm not crazy I'm miserable and regretting how I acted when I was crazy. I'd never exactly been Mr. Adventurous even when I was pissed but I was a complete hermit now. Even my tobacco had to be bought for me by people who could leave the house without being taken away in a black van. White van would've been more likely and I would have properly lost it thinking they were taking me away somewhere to kill me.

My delusions actually started getting worse after my Nana, it's what I call my Scottish grandmother, was diagnosed with cancer. I was devastated but I couldn't actually break out of my own madness for long enough to be there for her. My Nana and Papa had always been there to shelter me in case my Mum was going away for a bit and I couldn't bear to stay with my Dad. One of the happiest times of my life was staying with them in the Lake district, while my brothers went to Shetland. Two weeks of chocolate, kettle chips and Metal Gear Solid with my own room, being looked after by two of the nicest people anyone could have the fortune to meet. When she got sick I didn't hear about it right away, people were protecting me from it with good reason. When I heard for the first time I didn't think conspiracy or implant, I just felt very sad in the most sane frame of mind I'd known for a long time. My Nana had cancer, the thing that killed my Grandfather and like any sympathetic person I reacted. I tore into the spies listening in on me, tore into them about compassion, about mercy and leaving the grieving to their grief, but of course they did nothing as always. Had they done anything else I don't think I would've known, the problem with people that are in your head is that they're always with you.

Things aren't as bad now as they used to be, cancer is very treatable, in fact my Nana is fine now. I was glad that she recovered but it tore into me a bit too much, knowing absolutely and completely that someday not just them but my parents and everyone I loved was going to die. It's one thing to know it and another thing to know how it feels when it's upon you and as if life just wanted to really give me a kicking, a cat I'd known for many years died. She slowly lost her strength, barely able to stand at the end. We watched this once vibrant creature, to us a member of the family slowly die piece by piece as the life faded from her. Unlike most deaths, this was truly like watching the last grain of sand fall from the hourglass, she died not of an accident or of a disease, just the slow passing of time. I wasn't sure which was worse, knowing it was coming and having to watch them slip away or it all happening suddenly, until I found out. Layla, to whom I devoted a chapter, died shortly thereafter. She had been with us a while after the incident with the drain but her kidneys had started failing. We didn't know at all, in fact it was when we took her to the vet that we found out. I remember waking up to my mother telling me that she had died, she died at the vet's on the table because of a reaction to the anesthetic, her kidneys had been failing and she didn't have long left but I would've liked to say goodbye. I still wonder if her kidneys failed because of an infection she caught in that house, if I had reacted sooner to the noise I heard she might still be here or I could've at least prevented that nightmare. We always regret not doing more while friends and family are still with us, but somehow we can almost never seem to take the lesson to heart, we are a strange species indeed.

Layla and Sarah were dead, two of my cats and life-long friends. My Nana had recovered from cancer and I was suffering from psychotic delusions. It's a good thing I started seeing a therapist.

Chapter 14: The Doctor

I had been on medication and it was working to combat my depression, but I was still hallucinating like a wild monkey on acid laced with crack, violently. My therapist was quite different from most of the other therapists I'd seen before, different in the way that seeing her actually helped me. Therapy is like medication, you need the right type for the right person or else it may not make things better and might actually make things worse, but my new therapist was firstly much cleverer than the others and secondly not even slightly grating. I find everyone grating, even Enya, especially Enya, but I find everyone grating in some way or another and new people that I haven't learned to like I find impossible to get on with. This should never be the way with a therapist and what's more for someone so completely paranoid who never trusts anyone especially not when on a Schizoff I found I could actually trust her as well.

There are some things I had never even told my therapists before, reasons for being a completely deranged nutter, which if I couldn't talk about then therapy would be a waste of time, exacerbating the problem which was pretending these things had never happened. It was actually my therapist who convinced me to get sober, not by any grand intervention but by the simple question, "Why don't you stop?" This I had never considered before, that things making me more miserable and crazy than they were making me happy could just be stopped as if addiction was logical. For me however it was, logically anything that ultimately made me feel worse was failing to accomplish the one reason for taking them, therefore logically any short term discomfort from the lack of satisfying an addiction could not compare to the long term benefits of quitting. It was still tough of course, but I was determined and because I was so determined going back to drinking or smoking weed simply wasn't an availlable option leaving only dealing with it and the subsequent realities I had been fleeing.

Dealing is tough, withdrawal after years of drug abuse, two counts of PTSD, fear of death, fear of government, fear of being falsely accused of a crime, fear of dying at the hands of some homicidal homophobe, being bisexual, being human, death, disease, going crazy, being crazy, my delusions of grandeur, my delusions of worthlessness, my delusions of being followed, talking to myself, and of course psychotic hallucinations. If you start running you eventually get caught by all the things you are running from and on that day you will have a lot of things to face. I had been a very bad boy and life had handed me a rather large bill I couldn't pay. Unfortunately there was nothing left to do but get in the kitchen and start washing some dishes or die, those were the choices. The same way I faced down every problem, total refusal to look problems in the face until they go away, was how I solved this except that was just to give the pain time to fade, after the problems didn't seem so daunting I began to sort through them and solve them one at a time. Some had to be long term goals like PTSD which can't be solved hastily and some after a few weeks in therapy could be happily put away neatly in a cupboard instead of buried in a lockbox.

Therapy is the necessary step for anyone to regain their happiness and sanity, if you have a problem with therapy then keep your opinions to yourself unless you really think judging something you don't understand and criticizing it in ways that encourage people to avoid getting help is really a good idea, if you do eastern medicine may be for you so if you do get cancer treat it with a nice herbal bath and some Echinacea, otherwise respect the discoveries of western medicine, stop being a hypocrite and a fool and stop thinking you know better than the doctors who study these things for a living. Therapy is a good thing with a bad reputation and the people who need it most tend to be the people who give it such a bad name. I've never heard of a person who went crazy and killed people because he went to therapy, only police men who didn't get therapy and after one last incident that pushed them over the edge going off and murdering people, ripper style. When people think the cure is the poison and the poison is the cure then they are going to suffer before the end.

Well I wasn't an immortal god anymore which sort of sucked, life is kind of pesky when you're going to die and everything is chaos no matter how hard you try to make sense of it, but reality was probably the only way to face.... erm, reality. I had gone insane far too many times and as much as I wanted to get back to my education I couldn't go anywhere near chavs without risking multiple homicides or just looking like a deranged twat as I came to realise that would probably go down. I wanted to meet people but my paranoia had only melted down into a social anxiety disorder and I wanted a life but I was still terribly suicidal. Things weren't good, and I still thought I was being followed. My therapist really helped me get through things but I had more help when I finally asked for it.

Chapter 14: Sub Chapter: A Bit Late for an Early Intervention

Despite the title of the sub chapter, The Early Intervention Service really did help me a great deal. They listened to me spout my nonsense about being followed by helicopters and police vans and so on but they always tried to show me I was never the sort of person who'd believe anything without sufficient cause and all of my reasoning was somewhat...unreasonable. I hadn't actually questioned very much whether or not this actually could be a gigantic, ongoing delusion with multi-dimensional characters all with their own personalities and back-stories. All of my "evidence" was hearsay, it was speculation and most of all it was wrong. I kept hearing voices outside in the street, but there are always voices outside in the street. I heard more cars going down the road than usual, but roadways change and things get diverted. I heard helicopters going overhead a lot but maybe they were just taking aerial shots of the city, who knows, maybe in conjunction with the new road system. I was determined to make it all fit my pattern, but never willing to admit that not only might it not be unrelated that it could be connected but related to something completely unrelated to me. Just a few roadworks, diversions and aerial shots from helicopters to coordinate things. Plus I had never taken into account what I was doing when listening to voices from outside. They were always muffled and when something is muffled or you don't hear it properly your imagination fills in the blanks, some muffled shouting from a drunkard at 3AM turns into solid proof of a Totalitarian plot. Bollocks.

So yeah the EIS really helped me on that one and still do today. It's a shame the budget cuts are going to remove the service from operation when money is already drastically below what's needed for the mental health services. It's a huge problem, much more than people know and since most people just think it's an isolated problem and anyone in therapy is a nutter and anyone who's a nutter is somehow not a person, the problem persists. These services need more money otherwise trying to get people off benefit won't work. They need help not budget cuts and forced labour, still it's what we're all getting now. I have to write sodding books just to pay for my sodding smokes, I mean I'm too crazy to work and they'll get to my benefits eventually. Start trying to make a ridiculously crazy person who hates people and misuse of authority jump through hoops for some shitty person misusing his authority? I'd rather do what little work I'm capable of than that, hence working. Still I suppose they have that on their sides, the Conservatives, no other Government has forced this many crazy people to start trying to find ways to earn money just to avoid dealing with the stressful Jobseekers nonsense of having the lowest of the scum look down their nose at you because life dealt you a crappy hand. In all fairness to people working in benefits some of them are bloody good chaps, it's just some of them clearly don't want to be there and so take it out on everyone else there who incidentally also don't want to be there. Nobody wants to be there but we all dance our little dance so that for that one shining moment the tax man will actually shell out money himself as he pulls a shiny copper tuppence out of his pocket with his emaciated claws. I'm joking obviously, I'm always joking. Of course even when I was on Jobseekers the title was misnomer because I wasn't seeking a job because I was crazy and nobody bothered to explain things more clearly with regards to crazy people needing a whole other set of forms.

Pete was my worker and he helped me with everything from putting my delusions in context to figuring out what I wanted to do with my future now that I had one. Overcoming something that threatened to destroy your life is terribly difficult but once achieved no matter how much time you've lost the rest feels like nothing but gain, not all the time but it needs to be put in the proper perspective, like a deadly ailment your life seemed over and any more time you get to be happy or do something is a bonus. I'd lost my mind many times in various terrifying ways, but my battle with paranoid delusions was the closest I came to wearing a tinfoil hat.

Towards the end, I could see there was no compelling evidence but I still believed in my little conspiracy. To stop them getting into my mind using their mind control device I tried focusing on it to send a feedback loop that would overload the device, after all it was alien technology that couldn't be easily repaired and they would have to call in favours from Russia to bring in any more. I know, madness....

I didn't think I needed a thought shield because despite being crazy I always had a remarkable sense of control. It didn't matter how many times they used their thought control devices, I was neither easily swayed nor bothered by them glimpsing into my mind. They did so at their own peril after all, peril of seeing into my hell and for a second glimpsing their own, and even if that never happened I could always just overload their device again just to piss them off. Yes despite delusions usually overwhelming people to the point they feel no control I always managed to gain the upper hand and even in my delusional conspiracy world found a way to take control no matter how much my madness tried to shake me. Believing you're a powerful man is an illusion that can be shattered by a brief moment of madness. Believing you're a madgod is while harmful in its own right nothing any madness can break.

My therapist and my mental health team helped me break the grip of madness and trauma, it took a very long time something most people would rather try to skip over using a drink problem, and the knowledge of living in a world with terrible people which isn't something good people can ever accept, the only hope is simply to find a way either to confront it or just know it's there and not let it bother you too much. Turning to drugs and drink is going to land you in therapy eventually, just group therapy like AA or NA which for people who don't believe in God is more frustrating and painful than any trauma or worrying truth about the potential darkness of the human mind. So swallow your medicine and get the help you need or believe me, you will soon enough have your own story to write. Madness is terrible and terrifying but if you haven't suffered it's full might and force don't judge those who have, most of the time it doesn't happen because someone's weak or because they're naturally crazy, most of the time it happens because we live in a desperately depressing world where work drains you of all life and is the only way to survive, where dreams die because they are a risk unlike the 34th season of the second remake of a long running barely watched reality show. Life is business and business kills dreams, dreams are not good business because while they may be the most profitable when successful they aren't a risk anyone wants to take. We all want reruns and remakes and recycled newspapers, just the same old trash with barely a new thought because if there were ever a coherent thought it might actually make us think. We watch to forget and stop thinking because even the so-called strong among us work hard to maintain their ignorance or else face those things so terrible no man can stand strong before them, none but the mad, none but the truly strong, those who have faced demons and stood strong before them, those who no longer fear even death, those who do not boast strength because they have never been challenged but because they have been challenged and have overcome beasts most cannot perceive save in their darkest nightmares. We have faced living nightmares and won and now we live the waking dream. We stand before the darkness and we do not falter because there is nothing left to fear, we know what the world is and we know who we are, the thing that makes us free from oppression and free from tyranny, free from control and manipulation, free even from this prison called reality and free to return if it should suit us. Most only know what their eyes can tell them and their eyes tell them little, even of this world. A man with an imagination has eyes that can see beyond any world to any darkness or light others never can and because of it your notions of strength mean little to us because you never have and never will have any idea what's out there as soon as you close your eyes.

Chapter 15: Triple Strength Coffee and Cigarettes

Without drugs, real drugs anyway, I had to make do with what little I could be completely addicted to without it costing me my sanity. Triple strength coffee, because normal strength coffee just didn't have any punch to it, was pretty good at the time. When I started I didn't want to smoke any weed in case it made my anxiety and paranoia worse making huge amounts of coffee and staggering levels of caffeine and nicotine in my system the logical solution. Sleep, the famous alternative to passing out when the stimulants in your system just can't keep you awake any longer, I was never big on. Such a colossal waste of time to spend half your life not living it just for the purposes of processing information and preventing total madness and certain death. Sleep was a nice experience but spending it playing computer games seemed like a preferable option. I'd become a complete hermit but messing with my sleep just enough to reverse my entire bodily clock was probably the only way I was ever going to complete my transformation from lunatic to creature of the night. I could probably be mistaken for a vampire due to my repulsion to sunlight but night is the one time of day when you're almost guaranteed to be avoided, feared and left alone by all the ridiculous people who somehow think that their baseless opinions are of any merit, the one time you can ever be certain to complete a coherent thought without being bothered by some jackass who can't do it himself and doesn't want you to either. Sure the streets are usually filled with drunks but this I was accustomed to and by 3AM they've all wandered home, then for the next four hours I can indulge the wonderful illusion of being the only man on Earth besides those guys running the 24 hour off-license. I could walk around without fear in a world without social anxiety. The plague had struck and the clones were all dead and I was finally free, there may not have been any women in my life but that didn't make a change, I was at least finally without fear of being harassed because everyone else was dead, my dream had come true.

The night and living in it is a strange experience, the sun rising becomes your signal to go to sleep and as soon as the light stops hitting your eyes it's time to wake up to a world with no-one else in it. I didn't mind, conversation is for people who don't find themselves to be more than enough company and have the constant urge to remind people they're still here. I don't have that need, just the desire to be left alone because as soon as everyone else stops talking I finally start to feel happy. The strange thing about talking is that people who have the least to say tend to talk the most as if they think saying a lot is the same as having a lot to say. On the other hand people with a great deal to say tend never to speak, probably because people who have a lot to say tend to spend most of their time thinking and not speaking. The saying "I think therefore I am." seems oddly relevant, as if those who rarely think must struggle to be noticed by those who do or else begin to fade as soon as they're forgotten. This behaviour is classic immaturity, a baby fears death if it is not noticed so it cries whether it needs something or simply needs to know it's noticed, people who need to be the centre of attention still feel that they will somehow die if they don't keep forcing people to notice them, either that or they actually believe themselves to be so interesting people will gladly be interrupted just to hear them speak again.

The night is free from these problems and these people, just the cold, the dark and the deafening silence as you look up upon the stars, see the curving of the Earth's atmosphere and know as you look upon those distant lights not only are you seeing the past, but your own insignificance against the size and power of a star. The sky isn't what it used to be, those multicolored flashing lights have ruined the night's true beauty, the arc of the galaxy and those transcendental colors versus what few stars are still visible against that purple smog and the blinking light of a kebab shop sign. The raw power and beauty of existence was once readily visible to anyone who dared stare up at it, now all we can see are our own lights reflecting off the atmosphere and right back to where they started. It's no wonder we think we're the greatest thing in the Universe, we blocked out the one argument that speaks volumes against us, the Universe itself. I could enjoy the air without the taste of other people in it, the purity of life beyond people, but without the Universe being as visible as it used to the night sky was no more interesting than a television screen on snowstorm.

Coffee fueled nights kept me going. I will always despise people for the way they treat each other but as long as I could get some time to myself without having to worry about when the next person would try to get me to notice them, I could find some measure of peace. I've considered many times becoming a hermit, it certainly warrants consideration when people are currently a detriment to your life but are also worth nothing. They're noisy and stupid and think you actually want to know that they exist or that somehow you'll hear them shouting drunkenly and think, "Hey, that guy's being really noisy while drunk. He must be really interesting and intelligent not to mention a truly unique person who from this moment on I shall never forget nor shall I be able to compare this instance to any other." Then again expecting anything else from a drunken student is expecting blood from a stone. Technically that did happen that one time with that thing called life, but the improbability of a drunk student behaving in a manner which isn't an affront to public decency is roughly the same as the improbability of life occurring.

I used to be one, not a student but a drunk and an affront to public decency, but I did at least have the excuse of being completely miserable and insane. Most students only have the excuse of not knowing any better, acting like animals because they're treated like responsible adults without knowing how to act like responsible adults. I have met some students who didn't drink heavily and break laws but naturally they came to University to study and came to University from another country. We don't appreciate anything we have which is all the more sad because of how many people are exploited to give us everything. Cheap labour elsewhere makes us all better off and if we can't even appreciate it then we're spitting it the faces of the people who are already exploited. We should be ashamed for being so apathetic about our lives when we are fortunate enough to have the opportunity to be so whingey and pathetic. We don't know how good we have it so we don't care about anything but what we don't have. I personally am glad to have as much as my sanity or some measure of happiness knowing what it's like not to have those things, I'm glad I don't have a serious illness and I'm glad I have people who love me. I'm glad I have a home and I give money to the homeless, I'm glad I have enough food to eat and that I can be so picky as to decide what to eat and I'm glad to have clean drinking water, all these things are relative luxuries as are most of the things we think we need. I complained for years about not having a girlfriend in a world where people are dying from starvation. I was a whiny and ignorant piece of shit, but I've changed. I talk about how survival is not enough, but it is and anything else is a luxury and in a world this overpopulated we can either have luxury or equality, I know which one I want.

Chapter 16: The Universe

When we cannot see beyond ourselves, our wars, our ideals and our desires we see only ourselves reflected in what little of our world we can see and desire to inflict ourselves upon it. When you look upon the Universe and the cascade of galaxies and stars, when you look at the sheer immensity of it all that is so far beyond your comprehension it is to know not only that we are not all-knowing or all-seeing but to know that unfathomable depth reflected in you. That sight I could always see during the day, the people who sought to destroy me never could because their offenses meant nothing to the Universe and what meant something to me or what hurt my feelings was as insignificant as the movements of dust. Knowing this and understanding why it is so important to be good to one another because we only get one life and one chance, it made it obvious what my only choice was no matter how difficult it was at times. I had to be a good and decent person because all this would inevItably end, my life, our species, life, the planets, the stars, the galaxies and the Universe, and like with life we have to make the best of it while we're here and if we do so at the cost of others it is beyond selfish because it is not just other people who suffer the consequences but all of history is crippled for it. Some may want a rebirth of an empire and to become the ruler of the world, but as we all understand this is what we call an infantile fantasy, even if made reality and no matter how all-encompassing it cannot compensate for how limited the vision is, only one person gets to be free and billions of human lives are their toys and not even daddy is around to tell you what to do anymore so you don't even have to share, wow, what a stupid notion. So kindly step out of the way, real adults have things to do, you know, sciencey stuff.

Domination is the dream of all people who never grew up, real adults know that we're all in this together. Every tyrant throughout time has been the same, Peter Pan complex combined with juvenile fantasy and the power to kill anyone who said he wasn't really a big boy like daddy told him, the ridiculous notion that power to kill someone is the same as being right when all adults know that ideas you don't agree with are challenged in the arena of debate with the necessary impartiality to find the truth. I pity them in the most sincere sense of the word. They never had the chance it seems to become more than their fathers, but to know what it is in them you hate and become twice the man they ever could be, that is the answer, not to become him in an attempt to gain the love and respect he isn't capable of, not to spend your life chasing a lie, just tell him to fuck off and die and that you'll help him get there if necessary and remember who he was just enough to be nothing like him. Remember him by letting everything he believed in die, exactly what the bastard deserved.

So all that's left is to wrap up apparently, twenty three years barely made a short novel, humbling indeed. So I guess this is the part where I'm supposed to tell you how everything worked out okay. Sorry, but this isn't a film where he gets the girl and rides of into the sunset to live happily ever after. Life always has something more to throw at you and if it didn't it would get pretty dull, you don't magically fall in love just because you don't have any problems with madness anymore and you sure as hell don't get a six figure salary job from being a socially anxious high school dropout. Not that those things bother me anymore but you know how shallow people think happiness works. Sorry folks no big finish, but I'll try to make it good.

Chapter 17: The Death of The Green Jacket and The Great Bodhisattva

Before I finally put my madness behind me I had one last thing to do, I'd kept my old Green Jacket for many years, a keepsake but also a way of clinging onto the hope of one day saving the world. I never can now, all that youthful and revolutionary fire died after about the second guided tour of hell. But it was still important to me, important enough that I'd try to get it back unless I couldn't. It was a symbol to me of the hero I could be, but that possibility was never there, it was just another figment of my imagination, another delusion of grandeur. The Jacket itself was important to me, but what was more important was destroying the magic bound to it. When you pour your hopes and dreams and an entire world's fight for survival into an object it's said to imbue it not only with the spirit of the fight but with the power of the entire Universe you create around it. A truly powerful talisman that I didn't want to fall into the wrong hands. In case you actually believe in magic know this, you cannot destroy it, you cannot break a spell merely counteract it with another, all I really did was to release it. Concentrated power is the enemy of freedom, everything the Jacket was supposed to oppose so how could I let it exist if that's what it was? So I burnt it, fire is the only way with these things you see, but as I said the magic is not gone, that's the thing about magic it's never gone but there's only so much magic in the world and it's not right for a person to hoarde it, especially if it works. Maybe magic isn't what it used to be, but it's still here, in our lives and in our love instead of in the hands of a few magical men as the legends say. So maybe it was magic, maybe it wasn't, without a Magicometer I dare you to prove either way, for all we know magic is a sort of concentrated quantum flux, the behaviour of sub-atomic particles reacting to the will, perhaps it is, perhaps it's not and who really cares? I burnt the jacket and spoke a few mystical sounding words, enough said. It let me move on and quite frankly I don't care what else was real except that I really burnt it. The end.

So where do we go from here? That is up to you. Matrix of course, Neo, but who doesn't funking love that film. The first one isn't up for debate and for purposes of believing the world is a better place than it is my mind only recognizes one Matrix film, and four Star Wars films, in all honesty I liked Revenge of The Sith. Still this is selective and conscious denial, double think and it's perfectly benign because I know what the truth is and I even accept it, I just pretend not to for humour's sake. So what is the rest of my story, I don't know although likely you don't care. I'm fine really, no drugs and no drink, sober for over two years now. I haven't been delusional for six months and I'm actually starting to do something with my life. I've never had a girlfriend or boyfriend for that matter, I'm still pretty much alone but I have my family even without anyone else.

So every reason to be depressed, plus you know about my life being total madness and unpleasant madness at that. I have no job prospects, no love life and very few friends. But on the bright side, I'm a bisexual witch, a dimension bending Shaman, a homicidal maniac twice the size of most people, a killer who can't and will not kill, a Scottish man with all the inherent drawbacks and none of the soothing accent, a rebel with a cause but no rebellion, a Che Guevara look-a-like wearing a Che Guevara T-shirt, a philosopher without the necessary herum of women, a writer with no agent, and secret agent without an agency, and I think I'll be just fine, honestly there is nothing left for life to throw at me that can smack me with half the impact of the last boatload of anvils, I'm stronger, faster, better and I'm going to live a happy life. Oh and by the way, fight your own damn revolution for your own damn world, after all the shit I've been through, I've retired. I'm just going to sit on my arse and watch the sun set over this beautiful, twisted world...

I'm a 6'4" high school dropout, a writer whose ambition far exceeds his potential. I'm 23 going on a thousand and I've been to Hell and back. I've seen the face of God and I've known madness. I've met my heroes in one place or another. I speak to the dead and never to the living. I've faced vicious demons time and again and fought back government agents working for secret societies. I've destroyed government property and alien devices with the power of my mind and brought men of blind faith to see a little truth. I've taken a horse to water and I made the bastard drink. I've been places you can't imagine and while you'll never know what it means to be this sick I have understood how it feels to be you. Every person I meet is with me forever and so are thousands I've never met. I've seen ancient Egypt with my own eyes and stood atop a palace and looked out upon my kingdom, I've lived through time and space and known many things no mortal should ever know. I'm the Scorpion, the Lizard and the Phoenix, the hero, the villain, the drunk. I've known powerful ecstasy and smoked some potent skunk. I'm one of six billion, the last man on Earth and I'll live from my death til the day of my birth. True love is always fleeting but once I knew it well, true pain can last forever, the one enduring hell. I've known the best and worst of you and know I'm in between, not royal British beggar nor your lowly British Queen. I'm your saviour and your antichrist, your devil and your god, your Krishna and your Buddha, and on Krypton I'm called Zod. I'm no man, I'm every man, I'm fucking superman, and because I'm made of gingerbread just catch me if you can. I'm a whore and I'm a virgin and many other things, I'm a priceless artifact to many middle eastern kings. I'm just fucking with you if you see, cos what you think is what you be, and to everyone this golden rule applies. You're everything and nothing, you're everyone and no-one and you're nothing like you and everything like me. Personally, I'm alive, and for now, I can live with that.

of anvils, I'm stronger, faster, better and I'm going to live a happy life. Oh and by the way, fight your own damn revolution for your own damn world, after all the shit I've been through, I've retired. I'm just going to sit on my arse and watch the sun set over this beautiful, twisted world...

I'm a 6'4" high school dropout, a writer whose ambition far exceeds his potential. I'm 23 going on a thousand and I've been to Hell and back. I've seen the face of God and I've known madness. I've met my heroes in one place or another. I speak to the dead and never to the living. I've faced vicious demons time and again and fought back government agents working for secret societies. I've destroyed government property and alien devices with the power of my mind and brought men of blind faith to see a little truth. I've taken a horse to water and I made the bastard drink. I've been places you can't imagine and while you'll never know what it means to be this sick I have understood how it feels to be you. Every person I meet is with me forever and so are thousands I've never met. I've seen ancient Egypt with my own eyes and stood atop a palace and looked out upon my kingdom, I've lived through time and space and known many things no mortal should ever know. I'm the Scorpion, the Lizard and the Phoenix, the hero, the villain, the drunk. I've known powerful ecstasy and smoked some potent skunk. I'm one of six billion, the last man on Earth and I'll live from my death til the day of my birth. True love is always fleeting but once I knew it well, true pain can last forever, the one enduring hell. I've known the best and worst of you and know I'm in between, not royal British beggar nor your lowly British Queen. I'm your saviour and your antichrist, your devil and your god, your Krishna and your Buddha, and on Krypton I'm called Zod. I'm no man, I'm every man, I'm fucking superman, and because I'm made of gingerbread just catch me if you can. I'm a whore and I'm a virgin and many other things, I'm a priceless artifact to many middle eastern kings. I'm just fucking with you if you see, cos what you think is what you be, and to everyone this golden rule applies. You're everything and nothing, you're everyone and no-one and you're nothing like you and everything like me. Personally, I'm alive, and for now, I can live with that.

Epilogue

I'm just going to rant on a few more things, the book is over so if you want to stop feel free, I couldn't but that's just me.

Chapter Z: Survival of The Fittest

Most people who quote this term do so quite incorrectly. They use it as a term to justify the exploitation of others in whatever way they personally find most appealing. They believe perhaps that their savvy business sense perhaps makes them more worthy than perhaps the people whose hard work makes their job viable. Without them you can't survive, on the other hand they can survive and contribute without you, so if there's only one boat.... Survival of the fittest by process of natural selection to put it in proper context is not a process of exploitation in order to further your own ends at all because natural selection is another word for luck. Species depend upon nature's good graces for survival as warm winter coats do not bode well in harsh Arabian deserts, yet nature does not have "graces", nature is a fickle bitch however scientifically predictable she may be. The species that survive and those traits that carry forward are those traits that just so happen to be most useful at the time. Faster, stronger these things mean nothing to us now, their only uses are entertainment, a completely impractical purpose. Sure people try to exercise these traits as if they are still of value, trying to change the world so as not to be useless, but quite honestly you can't fuck the future, the future fucks you. The violent will not survive by intimidating people with violence. You can fight and struggle all you like but it's going to happen eventually and your useless little contribution to the gene pool will rapidly dry up.

It sounds cruel but this is in fact the indifference of natural selection or survival of the fittest, that useless traits cease to propagate themselves very rapidly after becoming useless and since people who most often misquote the sound theory of a great man are either morons or exploiters or quite probably both, they just happen to fit neatly into the population segment about to come to a grinding halt. You see, homosapiens survive for two reasons. Our two greatest survival tricks are intelligence, that which fostered all the discoveries that allowed us to survive beyond almost any natural disaster, and of course humanity. Humanity is that trait we most empathize with, it's compassion, justice and working together for the betterment of all our lives. Many species hunt in packs as they can fell greater feasts together and increase their survival chances, but we do much more than even chimpanzees. Chimpanzees themselves form groups not unlike tribes, a group of monkeys working together in similar social structures to our own civilization to increase their survival chances. Our ancestors formed similar tribes in order to survive the basis of which has always been to focus on our similarities instead of our differences. The single greatest truth of any human life is that no individual can survive without the support of the tribe, the tribe however can survive without an exploiter and in fact will thrive. We all, except psychopaths and sociopaths, understand that we are one family and that our similarities are more important than our differences. That moment when you see yourself reflected in another person. When you see that, the moment of empathy, you cannot kill them because they are not the enemy, the enemy is the voice telling you to kill. When you see yourselves in others and come to recognise your similarities and common interests, hurting them, exploiting them or even just standing by and watching someone else making them suffer becomes intolerable because you could no more stand it being done to them than to you.

This empathy with other people is the basis of all our greatest traits, compassion, self-sacrifice, charity, mercy, trust, love and friendship, they are the things heroes are made of which is why heroes inspire us so deeply. Without these things, the true traits not only of a great humanitarian but of a person who has humanity in even the smallest measure, without them you do not possess the only thing that makes us truly human. After all is it not sadism, brutality, murder, rape is it not these things we consider inhuman, the traits possessed by those who either do not know or do not care why these things are wrong, the people who don't see themselves in others and so don't care what happens to them in the slightest. People who take pleasure in the suffering of others know all too well that it's a person, they know they're causing pain and they revel in it. They must have some degree of empathy to understand the pain they're causing, but it is so twisted that to them pain in others is enjoyable, the more the better. It is a fine line between not caring about people you don't know and enjoying the suffering of people you don't empathize with, because they only have to irritate you once however unintentionally for it to push them from neutral into the ranks of the enemy. Can any of us honestly say that when someone we don't care about hurts us we don't try to hurt them back? We don't care to understand why it happened, we just want them to suffer maybe even more than they hurt us.

That I would say is the place you need to be to understand precisely why it is wrong. You have just been hurt and the pain and anger isn't going away, but as much as you hate feeling like that surely everyone else feels exactly the same when they've been hurt and maybe even take it out on someone else. I mean honestly is this all it comes down to? Someone hurts you because they've been hurt, and you hurt someone else or them, and then they hurt someone else, and they hurt someone else, and on and on for thousands of years until the entire world is constantly hurt and miserable, we don't think about how things affect others so we just escalate until the world becomes a shithole of a place to live? Surely if that's the problem then the solution is as simple as not taking out your anger on others and simply finding a constructive way to deal with it instead of a destructive way. I mean if everyone stopped taking their anger out on everyone else tomorrow, the world might stop being such a misery all the time, then again if you're a sadist you're probably liking things just the way they are and having a great deal of fun hurting people.

Chapter X: Bodhisattva Path

The Bodhisattva path is what I would call it. To those of us who understand, or at least those of us who think we understand, enlightenment is not enough. Many would say if enlightenment is not enough then you have not reached enlightenment, even if I were speaking to someone who had achieved enlightenment my answer would still be, you do not understand. To someone who had achieved enlightenment this comment would seem to be in error, a comment from someone who himself does not understand what enlightenment is. I do understand enlightenment, I have achieved enlightenment and it is not enough. From an enlightened perspective, there is no self, there is no pain and no fear, positive and negative are the same and neither is true for both are void which is all that is. Everything is void, without the definitions we assign there is no difference and this is the similarity all things share and the basis of all existence. It is not unlike energy from a scientific perspective, as all matter and perhaps everything which interacts with matter are made from, this however would be unlike the energy we see interacting with our environment from the kinetic based energy of heat or an object in motion beyond the collapse of the wave function, or indeed even the "potential energy" found in the chemical bonds between atoms or an object at distance from the center of gravity of an object of sufficient mass, it would follow many of the same rules, it can be neither created nor destroyed but only transforms from one form to another, however the interactions between energy and matter we can observe are far removed from energy as it is in it's pure yet inactive state. I apologize for the speculation but I make it purely for the sake of illustration, void is not only when something ceases to be anything, it is also what everything always is and when we see definition or observe differences, that is the illusion.

This enlightened mindset really isn't enough though, quite frankly if you no longer view suffering as something that exists, if to you all suffering is an illusion then you alone can find peace in that knowledge. Meaning is a human derived concept, we created the idea and without us or the perception of its existence in the truest sense it does not exist. If even one man believes something to have meaning, it has meaning for he alone can make that decision. If one person alone believes something matters then it matters because whether other people can see it or not, whether they believe it or not, it matters. The same is true of suffering, if someone believes they are an individual self apart from the world then they are, if they believe suffering is terrible and do not wish it inflicted upon them it is real and would cause them terrible distress, if a person believes something is real then it is real because nothing is more or less real than when it is perceived to be so. Despite what enlightenment tells us, there is no suffering, acceptance, inner peace, there is no amount of inner peace or denial that will make their suffering any less real. We cannot decide what is real to them, it is a betrayal of everything Buddhism stands for, therefore we can only conclude that as long as someone, anyone believes in and experiences suffering then it is still just as real as before we realised it was illusion. We are one, in my opinion the greatest lesson of Buddhism, but the lesson is not that if one achieves enlightenment we all do, clearly that is not the case, you may be the Universe, you may be existence, but existence is in pain and whether you feel it or not does not change the fact that we are one and if even one suffers we must all suffer with them. Enlightenment is a one man escape pod, the Bodhisattva path is for the truly courageous of spirit.

When I speak of the Bodhisattva path I don't actually mean getting everyone to enlightenment. That would be kind of boring wouldn't it? It may sound like a strange statement from a supposed enlightened Buddhist, but then again I always found Star Trek more interesting than the teachings of Buddha. In essence the word Nirvana means cessation, it is an ending, not only the end of your suffering but of yourself. Here on planet Earth we have a word for the ending of your "self", we call it death. Even the word cessation implies that it is the end and maybe there is a magical cloud city full of the enlightened all agreeing with each other all the time, but even if there is it does sound peaceful, blissful but I crave excitement. What can I say? I'm a drama queen. Nonetheless, I don't think I'd be okay with no more excitement, no more fun, no more danger and intrigue and mystery. And what about me, I like me, without a self I'm not me anymore I'm just everyone else and no-one. So I don't even think a world of enlightened people is a good idea, I mean the whole idea is just that we should all leave because this place is shit. It can be, but not always. Life can be fun and joyous, there's even love to speak of and without the idea of self there can be no love for an individual, not that love we dream of, only the love for all known as compassion. Nor without self can there be self-sacrifice. It is a dangerous idea when taken to its conclusion especially since when you achieve true enlightenment even your sense of self-preservation goes silent. Life or death, eat or starve, with the mental discipline to make your understanding your complete reality it is clear these things do not matter and you won't care to act as if they do. Understanding what reality truly is, it's more dangerous than most people realise and unless you spend years preparing for it, you might not take it well.

Dark enlightenment, that's when without training to shut out the negative, self-destructive thoughts, enlightenment becomes a nightmare. Without proper meditation and self-discipline and without the constant expectation of something glorious and blissful enlightenment can have just the wrong spin for some people. Usually a horrendous wretch of a person, a deeply poisoned and hateful being, a selfish egotistical know-it-all, a victim who revels in his own suffering, not unlike myself of course, on all four counts. I was proud and I was foolish, I was young and in too much of a hurry, I thought I was exceptional and therefore rules were just there for other people too stupid to know why rules were there. I deserved what I got, and it was hell. Nothing quite compares, though I have heard some things can be worse, to having your soul ripped out. To most it's like blending, becoming a part of the Universe and everything in it truly and completely, you feel it and you know it, but I was rather attached to my ego and I didn't let it go willingly. It felt like the Universe was screaming and everything turned dark. To know hell is to know utterly and undeniably that everything you hoped was utterly false and everything you feared was completely true. Everything seems to get turned upside down, the world isn't infinite in complexity and diversity and every new moment isn't a chance for something great, the wheel turns and nothing changes but the wheel will never stop, it just keeps turning as you watch nothing happen forever. There is no saving humanity, they will all die, the stars will die, the Universe will die and it will all be forgotten, nothing means anything, there is no meaning to anything and there never can be. It's all completely pointless and that's all it will ever be. Nothing lasts forever except your suffering as you watch helpless as everything inevitably dies, though it doesn't matter. Joy, sadness it's all the same thing so even when you're happy you are invariably miserable and that's what you'll feel, and it's all nothing, no change, no differences, it's all just the same fucking thing over and over again like the same piece of grey cardboard passing in front of your eyes until you go completely insane.

That was my Dark enlightenment. Personally, I want love and I want spaceships. So forget about your cheap copy of a Buddhisty book on synchronicity, you can make someone happy today instead. Suck some cock, eat some pussy, or both if you shwing the way I do, or maybe just eat a pie and watch some TV. It's all good, and the spaceships are coming.

Chapter Y: Zero Point

Zero point, no matter how long we survive and how much we've learnt there is always something more to deal with. The definition of Zero Point, not zero point energy, in my definition at least is the point when all that is learnable has been learnt, everything has been discovered and every possible divergence of history has been known. Times of great peril and safety, times of great trial and of great reward, when all things have passed, all trials have been overcome. The day there are no more problems except for our problem with there being no problems. It sounds like an impossible thing, but it's inevitable in a few billion years that there will simply not be anything left for us. In thousands of years alone we have discovered almost everything we can think of, and on the day there are no more scientific discoveries, the scientists will cease to be, the nurses and the doctors when illness is nothing but a memory, when there is nothing left to learn and nothing left to teach because men who live almost indefinitely can lose their taste for life, when there is no more joy to life and no more struggle to let us know the difference, we will die simply because there is no reason left to live. Eventually, no matter what, we must come to an end and our memory may be nothing more than a curse to any who know what it means to be victorious as a species. We must end inevitably and we must be forgotten because it doesn't matter whether we die and are forgotten, just that someone else gets to live without our shadow cast over their life. The Native American saying, Enjoy Life's journey but leave no tracks, is what I mean because while our egos wish to be remembered it is not something we can have. We pass from memory and recognition as the tide washes in, but it's okay because someone else will get the chance to live and learn everything anew. No memory of science or philosophy, just a brand new adventure, a brand new story. To be sad for ourselves is foolish as nothing can be done, we must instead focus on the certainty and be happy for those who will live and learn and love, making their own history and their own lives mean something and painting their own pictures on their own sky. It's nothing to fear, just the knowledge that no matter how long it takes life will come back is enough for me to accept that eventually, this light can go out, before it no longer illuminates our existence and casts only a shadow. Any event however unlikely occurs finitely over a finite length of time no matter how unbelievably long. The beginning of a Universe, the beginnings of life, anything and everything that's possible. Life is not infinitely improbable, we have a word for that, impossible, when you are infinitely close to zero chance you are at zero chance, we are here so it is not impossible. Any improbable event occurs finitely over a finite length of time, but energy is infinite in time and capacity, any improbable event becomes certain over an infinite length of time and in fact occurs infinitely, in other words, like hope, Life Springs Eternal.

www.ingramcontent.com/pod-product-compliance
Ingram Content Group UK Ltd.
Pitfield, Milton Keynes, MK11 3LW, UK
UKHW041412180426
11947UKWH00007B/75

9 781849 915878